COMPLETELY
FRANK
THE LIFE OF FRANK
SINATRA

DEBORAH HOLDER

BLOOMSBURY

For my family

First published in Great Britain 1995
Bloomsbury Publishing Plc, 2 Soho Square,
London W1V 6HB

A CIP catalogue record for this book
is available from the British Library

ISBN 0 7475 1979 X

10 9 8 7 6 5 4 3 2 1

Picture Sources:
Advertising Archives: 64; Archive Photos: 14, 17, 18 (bottom), 33 (bottom), 54 (top),
60 (top left, bottom), 65 (top), 75 (top left), 110 (bottom), 117 (top), 132, 168,
169; Associated Press: 69; Aurora: 178; Frank Driggs Collection: 13, 23 (top), 25
(bottom), 26, 27, 31, 33 (top), 35, 36, 37, 38, 40/1, 45 (bottom), 49 (bottom), 54
(bottom), 63, 66, 129; Hulton Deutsch: 119, 167, 171; The Kobal Collection: 1, 8, 52,
59 (bottom), 65 (bottom), 70 (left), 71, 72 (bottom), 73 (bottom), 77 (bottom), 82,
83, 86, 90, 93, 102/3,104, 108 (bottom), 109 (top), 112, 114, 124, 125 (left),
127, 130, 147, 149 (top), 151, 153, 155 (bottom), 156, 157, 184; Martin Mills:
141; Pictorial Press Ltd: 21, 59 (top), 62, 133; Popperfoto: 81; Range/ Bettmann: 30,
39, 42, 43, 44, 45 (top), 51, 55, 57, 58 (bottom), 61, 67, 68, 76, 78, 85, 87, 88,
110 (top), 115, 117 (bottom), 118, 120, 121, 126, 134, 135, 137, 138, 155 (top),
159, 160, 162, 166 (bottom), 172, 173, 176, 177, 179 (top); Redferns: 32, 77
(top), 100 (bottom), 111, 122, 123, 131, 139, 150, 163, 164/5, 174, 179
(bottom), 182, 183; Rex Features: 20, 29, 46 (top), 58 (top), 75 (bottom), 80, 97,
142/3, 152, 161, 168 (top), 171, 180, 181; Sipa Press: 175; Snap-Photo/ Katz: 28,
34, 49 (top), 60 (top right); Stills: 22; Bob Willoughby: 70, 89, 91, 92, 95, 105, 106,
107, 148/9

Design and picture editing by
Simon Jennings & Amanda Allchin
Jacket design Simon Jennings
Cover photograph by Huw Nichols
Typesetting in Futura condensed & Bodoni poster
Picture research by Anne-Marie Ehrlich
Printed by Graphicon SRL, Italy

Acknowledgements

Too young to have seen Sinatra live in his prime, I am indebted to Braveworld Video whose loan of *The Sinatra Collection* (volumes 1 – 12) enabled me to see what all the fuss was about. Many thanks also to the British Film Institute and the Sinatra Music Society for their expertise, and to the many excellent biographers whose books helped me piece together Sinatra's sixty year career.

On a more personal note I would like to thank Jonathan Coe for a much-appreciated leg-up and also Crouch End's answer to Mary Poppins, Siobhan Sneddon Kay, for keeping my children at bay. I am also extremely grateful to friends and family for their encouragement, and to Joseph Navin in particular for his invaluable advice and support. And last but not least, thanks to Mr Sinatra for making it easy by having talent and personality in spades.

CONTENTS

Introduction

"Whatever else has been said about me personally is unimportant. When I sing I believe I'm honest . . . the audience is like a broad — if you're indifferent, endsville."

In his heyday Francis Albert Sinatra was known simply as The Voice; recognized by his peers — songwriters, critics, arrangers and musicians — as the greatest singer of his generation. What made him stand out in the beginning, and continues to transcend his failing vocal skills at almost eighty, is his unique ability to interpret a lyric, to get inside a song and make it his own. As a singer and performer he is second to none.

Does it matter, then, that the individual can be an arrogant tyrant unable to accept the slightest criticism, a bully whose abusive behaviour to those around him can be merciless and cruel? Right or wrong, the conflict between the sensitive artist and the crass individual is so marked that it becomes the most striking thing about Sinatra, so much so that the public persona has frequently threatened to overshadow his talents on stage and screen. This is particularly true for my own generation — the under-forties with no first-hand experience of Sinatra in his prime — but has applied to some extent throughout his career. When he became a teen idol long before Elvis, his fans caused rioting in the streets, but it was about his tangled love affairs and temper tantrums that the public wanted to read. As a swinging bachelor a decade later he ruled the charts, but it was reports of his violent excesses and Mob connections that governed the headlines. The same problems ended his friendship and political involvement with the Kennedys in the Sixties and soured his emergence from retirement in the Seventies. Even his triumphant comeback at the Academy Awards in the Fifties was upstaged by his affair with Ava Gardner. From all this emerges a Sinatra who is far easier to admire than he is to like and this paradox lies at the heart of any attempt to assess his life and career.

Unfortunately, Sinatra rose to fame in the days of the all-powerful studios, when an actor signed away his private life when he signed his contract. In their wake came the increasingly popular tabloid press with its insatiable appetite for celebrity gossip and refusal to let the facts get in the way of a good story. But although fame has dictated that his life be acted out in public, Sinatra has stubbornly refused to play the game: there have been many biographies, but none of them authorized, a move that has inadvertently fuelled speculation; he has regularly attempted to sue for invasion of privacy but always behaved in a way guaranteed to attract attention; and he has built up a hatred of the press that is so intense he virtually provokes attack. In short, he is his own worst enemy. Worse still, he is fighting a losing battle because, whether he likes it or not, Sinatra the man and Sinatra the singer are inseparable. The paradoxes are part of the appeal and the emotional extremes that make him a difficult man are the same ones that make him a great singer.

Finally, Sinatra the man has added fascination because in many ways he personifies the American Dream. His rise from humble immigrant beginnings to a level of fame usually occupied by royalty is an integral part of his public persona. To have reached this point then lost everything before making the most spectacular comeback in show-business history makes for a life story even Hollywood couldn't have dreamed up. Most importantly, and quite incredibly given his regal behaviour, a part of Sinatra has always remained the archetypal ordinary Joe, a man to whom his audiences could relate. The key is his choice of material. Sinatra always looked for a meaningful narrative in a song, beginning with the greats of Tin Pan Alley – Berlin, Gershwin, Porter, Rodgers – then seeking out their successors in the same idiom – Sammy Cahn, Jule Styne, Jimmy Van Heusen, Johnny Mercer. As a result, his music became a reflection of his emotional ups and downs and his audience came to feel they knew him well. As he staggered to his prop bar stool, bruised by lost love, his jacket slung over his shoulder, a smouldering cigarette in one hand and a Jack Daniels in the other, he took his audience down with him. When he bounced back as the swinging bachelor in a snap-brim hat, his flamboyant optimism and cocky swagger raised the roof.

In the end, the songs should speak for themselves. Everyone has their favourites — the dark desperation of "I'm a Fool to Want You" or the bitter-sweet "In the Wee Small Hours of the Morning", soul-searching mini-dramas like "One For My Baby" and "Angel Eyes", the buoyant, uplifting Capitol classics, "You Make Me Feel So Young", "Come Fly With Me" or Cole Porter's quintessential "I've Got You Under My Skin" and "I Get A Kick Out of You" — there are so many to choose from. Whatever you think about Sinatra the man, it's impossible to listen to Sinatra the singer without feeling that this is as good as it gets.

CHAPTER ONE

RADIO DAYS, 1915

Hollywood, 1955. The glittering première for *Guys and Dolls* should have been a moment of glory for forty-year-old Frank Sinatra. The film was the latest of a clutch of much-needed successes. After sinking to a personal and professional nadir, the Chairman of the Board was back in business. It was, said *Variety* "the greatest comeback in theatre history".

Only a few years earlier Sinatra hadn't been able to get past the door at the major studios. His name, once a magnet for thousands of screaming bobbysoxers, was box-office poison. His wife of many years had finally divorced him and the explosive love affair that ended his marriage had itself finished in disaster. Most surprising of all, the singer whose success had once seemed unshakable had been unable to get a recording contract.

The recovery started in 1953 with *From Here to Eternity*, the film credited with singlehandedly hauling Sinatra's ailing movie career back from the brink. He carried off an Academy Award for his performance and went on to make more films in the mid Fifties than any other star in Hollywood, as well as recording some of his finest albums.

But although Sinatra should have been revelling in his return to form that night, the première was marred by his chronic insecurity and hypersensitivity to anything he interpreted as criticism, feelings that dogged him throughout his career. In this instance he was infuriated by the programme notes. "After soaring to what was almost national adulation a dozen years ago," they read, "a combination of poor roles, a bad press and other things sent his career zooming downwards. He was reputedly washed up. Today his second career is in high gear."

Sinatra stubbornly refused to see his success as a comeback — although it clearly was. The suggestion that he had hit rock bottom was an unacceptable blow to his pride. For others, the comeback

Frank Sinatra's first publicity shot, taken in 1938. He was eighteen and clearly under the influence of idol Bing Crosby.

An early portrait of Francis Albert Sinatra aged three, complete with dandyish top hat. Nine years earlier his parents, Natalie "Dolly" Garavanti and Anthony Martin Sinatra, tied the knot. Frank was to be their only child.

typified Sinatra the survivor. It was precisely the image he rejected that appealed to the public: the myth of the skinny kid from Hoboken who had dragged himself out of the gutter not once but twice. Throughout Sinatra's career, those responsible for his public image happily cashed in on his archetypal rags-to-riches story. The truth is even more interesting.

As the only child of a lower-middle-class family, Frank Sinatra was spoiled. From early on he was accustomed to getting what he wanted and having more than those around him. The person who shaped and provided for Sinatra's high expectations was his mother, Dolly. She was a formidable woman and the patterns she instilled in him lasted a lifetime.

Two conflicting pictures emerge from neighbourhood reminiscences of Dolly Sinatra: one, of a foul-mouthed, selfish and domineering figure, who put her own social aspirations before the care of her child; the other of a woman whose intelligence, self-confidence and ambition put her twenty years ahead of her time.

In the early years of the twentieth century, Italian immigrants arrived in the promised land at a rate of over a million a year. After landing in New York, many, like Dolly's mother and father, settled on the outskirts of the city. Dolly's proud Genoese parents had high hopes for their daughter, but it wasn't in Dolly's make-up to listen to others: she chose as her husband an illiterate boxer from Sicily. On Valentine's Day 1914, against her parent's wishes, Natalie Della Garavanti married Antonio Martin Sinatra. As Dolly set up home in the heart of Little Italy, the tough dock area of Hoboken, New Jersey (used as the backdrop for Elia Kazan's *On the Waterfront*), Italian immigrants were at the bottom of the heap. Both the Germans and the Irish were more successfully integrated and economically more powerful. Unlike many Italians, easily branded "wops" by their dark features, blonde, blue-eyed Dolly regularly passed herself off as Irish. Many people knew her as O'Brien and her husband fought under the name of Marty O'Brien.

Initially it was Dolly's flair for languages that made her an important figure in the tight-knit community where few spoke English with confidence. She became a go-between, always on hand when people needed help dealing with the American system. Her community work soon led to politics. She became a committed Democrat and went on to become the first immigrant woman to hold an official ward post, providing a natural link between Irish politicians and Italian voters, bound together by their immigrant status and Catholic beliefs.

On 12 December 1915, Dolly gave birth to her only child, Francis Albert Sinatra. The dramatic birth was strangely prophetic. Born breech at a massive thirteen-and-a-half pounds, Sinatra had to

Young Frank with his mother. While his father Marty remained on the sidelines, Frank and Dolly shared a very close relationship which remained significant until her death in 1977.

be torn from his mother's womb with forceps, leaving him with a badly damaged ear and deep scars on the left side of his face and neck. Legend has it that Sinatra was initially left for dead by the doctor, who then set about saving the mother. It was Dolly's own mother, Rosa Garavanti, who revived the bloodied baby by dousing him under a cold tap. Only minutes old, Sinatra had established himself as a survivor. Dolly subsequently brought him up to believe he had been saved for something great.

Dolly's work left her little time for mothering. As well as her political activities, she ran a saloon during Prohibition, acted as an official court interpreter and operated as a local midwife and abortionist. By all accounts she was also something of a party animal and often used medical call-outs as an excuse to go drinking, leaving the less gregarious Marty at home. All in all, her commitments meant Frank spent much of his childhood in the care of his grandmother, Rosa.

Beyond a genuine social bent, Dolly had her own aspirations. By the time Frank was twelve, she had engineered their first move uptown, away from the Italian neighbourhood and towards the wealthier Irish area. Moving upmarket meant dressing the part and Dolly saw to it that Frank was the only kid in the neighbourhood with his own account at the local department store. He became such a sharp dresser that he was known locally as Slacksey O'Brien. For an upwardly mobile immigrant, clothes were a badge of respectability and class, something which stayed with Sinatra through adulthood.

His mother's frequent hand-outs meant Sinatra developed an early cynicism where money was concerned. Money meant not only friends but protection in the gang culture of a rough neighbourhood. Sinatra always cut a particularly frail figure and learned early to surround himself with bigger boys.

Emotionally, Frank was not so well off. He was lonely and isolated: an Italian on Irish territory, the son of a high-powered working mother in a traditionally macho culture; an only child with cash in his pocket, surrounded by families of twelve without shoes on their feet. When his mother was arrested following an abortion in which a woman almost died, the local Catholic community was scandalized and Frank was further alienated. Undaunted by the social stigma, Dolly continued to practise.

Despite Dolly's encouragement, Frank never shone academically. Teachers described him as lazy, with "no real talent for anything". He lasted only a few months at high school before falling into a series of menial jobs. His lack of formal education was not something he worried about then, but in later life it would contribute to the monumental chip on his shoulder.

Where Sinatra's determination sprang from is hard to say. He

Echo Farm House in the Catskill Mountains, upstate New York, the Sinatra family's favourite holiday retreat. Frank, aged eight, sits surrounded by friends and relatives, including his mother who sits at his shoulder, guitar in hand.

wasn't guided by any strikingly obvious talent; indeed he was rarely taken seriously in his early years and it was only his own conviction that kept him going. After high school, he organized school dances. Using as leverage a PA and expensive orchestrations financed by Dolly, he was occasionally allowed to sing, but certainly wouldn't have stood a chance otherwise.

There were some musical influences at home — Dolly often sang at political rallies and weddings, and Frank's paternal grandfather, who gave him a ukulele for his fifteenth birthday, is said to have had a wonderful voice — but little to explain Frank's driving self-belief. According to Sinatra himself, one of the turning points was seeing Bing Crosby on the stage of the Jersey City vaudeville theatre in the early Thirties. "He had such a great ease that I thought, if he can do it that easily, I don't know why I can't."

Pretenders to the Crosby throne were a dime a dozen in the Thirties, but most imitators never escaped the clubs and bars. Sinatra knew he would have to be different. In fact he credits the highly idiosyncratic Billie Holiday, whom he had heard in 52nd Street clubs four or five years earlier, as his "greatest single musical influence".

Frank sang where he could for the next few years. "If the local orchestras wanted to use my arrangements — and they always did, because I had a large, up-to-the-minute collection — they had to take the singer Sinatra too. Nobody was cheated. While I wasn't the best singer in the world, they weren't the best bands in the country either." When his mother furnished him with a car he made himself useful to a local band, the Three Flashes, driving them to gigs and occasionally providing the vocals.

To his mother's disappointment Frank dropped out of Demerest High School early, later describing his brief academic career as "very uninteresting".

The proud parents. Dolly, the driving force behind both men, was responsible for Frank's first break and her husband's appointment to the fire department.

By the time Frank was twenty little had changed and it was time for Dolly to pull a few strings. Sinatra was not considered much of a singer, but nobody in Hoboken said no to Dolly. With her help, the Three Flashes were transformed into the Hoboken Four just in time for the group to take part in one of the more popular talent shows of the day, Major Bowes' Amateur Hour. They did well enough to be invited to tour with the Major's mixed bag of acts. Amidst much resentment, which resulted in serious bullying by two members of the band, Sinatra began to shine as lead vocalist. The more popular he became as a performer and an onstage ladies' man, the more often he was beaten. After three months he returned home, claiming homesickness.

After a spell spent singing at weddings and clubs and badgering radio stations for exposure, he found work at the Rustic Cabin, a local road house. For fifteen dollars a week he waited tables and acted as Master of Ceremonies for the house band, with whom he was also allowed to sing.

The Rustic Cabin's main appeal was the fact that it was hitched up to WNEW Radio in New York. Once a week the Harold Arden band was broadcast live from the Rustic Cabin as part of the *Saturday Dance Parade*. Jimmy Rich, an organist who often accompanied WNEW singers, remembered Sinatra's early determination: "Frank always seemed to make himself available whenever there'd be an opening. He was a pusher, always polite, but always interested in himself, too. I would come out of my office and he'd be standing there to see the head of continuity or anybody who would listen to him. Somehow he'd get past the reception and he'd be there." It took eighteen months of pushing before his voice was heard by someone who could take his career into a different league.

During the Thirties, radio was the main source of home entertainment. Times were hard and it offered cheap, accessible companionship. Bing Crosby sympathized with "Brother, Can You Spare a Dime?" and the optimistic enthusiasm of the Swing Era's big bands — Benny Goodman, Count Basie, the Dorseys, Glenn Miller — provided a temporary escape from the grim realities of the post-Depression years. The public took popular music to its heart and made stars of its favourites: top dog Crosby, with his easy delivery, relaxed persona and gentle, romantic melodies, and Dick Powell, the handsome tenor whose good looks led on to a film career. This was where Sinatra wanted to be and radio was where he would start.

The next step was records, an industry that was growing at an amazing rate in response to an insatiable public appetite. During the Thirties the market trebled, reaching sales of 33 million by the time Sinatra arrived on the scene and hitting a staggering 127 million by

Always the snappiest dresser on the block, Frank quickly developed his own style. It was wife Nancy, a prudent housekeeper, who made his famous floppy bow ties by hand.

The Hoboken Four pose with a local theatre manager. Frank (far right) quit the 50 dollar a week job after serious bullying by band members. Only a few years later he would earn over 2,500 dollars a week at venues like the Paramount Theatre and the Waldorf.

1941. The popularity of romantic singers continued to soar during the lonely war years. Sinatra's timing could not have been better.

Trumpeter Harry James was relaxing between performances at the New York Paramount Theatre when he happened to hear Sinatra on the local radio station. What caught his interest was Sinatra's "way of talking a lyric". It was 1939 and James had recently left the Benny Goodman band to start up on his own. He needed a vocalist to complete the line-up. Star vocalists had become something of a necessary evil for bandleaders. Competition was keen and a distinctive sound was important. Vocalists who could provide a more intimate, emotional connection with the audience, in contrast to the driving power of the band, were in great demand. Ella Fitzgerald was snapped up by Chick Webb's band, Benny Goodman featured Martha Tilton and later Peggy Lee, Billie Holiday teamed up with Count Basie and now James had found his man.

After hearing the broadcast, James visited the Rustic Cabin. "He'd only sung eight bars when I felt the hairs on the back of my neck rising," said James later. "I knew he was destined to be a great vocalist." In June 1939 Sinatra stepped on to the stage of the Hippodrome Theatre in Baltimore to make his début appearance with Harry James and his Music Makers. From there they moved on to the Roseland Ballroom in New York City for the summer season.

The reviews were good and Sinatra's "pleasing vocals" and "easy phrasing" got a special mention in *Metronome*, a leading music magazine. Although the journalist later admitted that he had been begged to put in a good word for the new vocalist, he had stumbled upon Sinatra's most enduring talent. Even before Sinatra had found and developed his style, his phrasing stood out. It began as a natural talent he didn't understand himself, but was something he was encouraged to build on. As he told *Life* magazine years later, in 1965, "It's just like reading poetry. And that's odd because poetry bores me. It always has. But when I do a song, I find that I enjoy it, and I find that I understand the distance necessary per phrase."

Just a few months before he joined Harry James, the twenty-four-year-old singer had married Nancy Barbato. The bride wore white and Dolly shed an obligatory tear. It was all she could have hoped for, but it hadn't been easy. As soon as Dolly had done what she could to kick-start her son's singing career she had turned her attention to his private life. There had been some initial problems, including a night behind bars for Sinatra when his then fiancé, Toni Delle Pente Francke, discovered his plan to marry another woman and charged him with adultery. Although the charges were eventually dropped they came back to haunt Sinatra on more than one occasion.

Having despatched the working-class divorcee as wholly

Although skinny and slightly jug eared, an abundance of confidence and style gave Sinatra the makings of a teen idol.

Anybody who was anybody played the Steel Pier, Atlantic City. In 1939, the recently formed Harry James Orchestra arrived with new vocalist Frank Sinatra, seen to the right of band leader Harry James and fellow singer Connie Haines.

unsuitable for her son, Dolly was prepared to make do with Nancy. She was ordinary and unthreatening, a devout Italian Catholic from a respectable family. From Frank's point of view she was prepared to put her own needs to one side and support him in the wholly uncritical way he demanded. He had made it known that he didn't want a woman who would get in the way of his ambitions and Nancy understood this well. Although it was a marriage in name only for all but the first few years, Nancy offered Frank a sense of long-term emotional security and family that kept him coming back as a friend and father long after their divorce.

They set up home in a three-room flat in Garfield Avenue, New Jersey. Nancy worked as a secretary and Frank at the Rustic Cabin. Between them they earned a decent wage, although a large chunk was needed to keep up with Sinatra's passion for sharp suits and silk bow ties. Nancy was the model wife, encouraging Sinatra to pursue his career even if it meant she saw little of him. She cooked a great spaghetti and worked hard to maintain a strained relationship with her mother-in-law.

The two men closest to Sinatra were Nick Sevano, who had been delivered by Dolly and had grown up alongside Frank in Hoboken, and Hank Sanciola, Sinatra's would-be manager. Sanciola had grown up on the mean streets of the Bronx and was a handy man to have around. Through his contacts in the business he got hold of new songsheets and music for Sinatra, put his name about, booked club dates for him and also provided the kind of muscle-bound presence Sinatra found so reassuring.

Conditions were perfect for Sinatra to thrive. Nancy catered for his domestic needs while his cronies dealt with business. As his reputation grew so did his entourage, with the result that he lived an increasingly cosseted existence surrounded by people prepared to take care of everything from laughing at his jokes to buying his shirts and occasionally fighting his battles for him.

With the growing public enthusiasm for the big bands' star vocalists, it was only a matter of time before popular singers hijacked the limelight from the orchestras that had launched and nurtured them. Songwriters could see which way the wind was blowing and were applying themselves to producing material for singers just like Sinatra.

At the height of the summer of 1939, Sinatra stepped into the studio for the first time. He recorded "From the Bottom of My Heart" and "Melancholy Mood", although as a mere band vocalist his name didn't feature in the credits. *Variety* pronounced the single to have "little appeal". It was still early days for James and his team — they had been together only nine months. Despite James's reputation as a

trumpeter, they had yet to make their name as a band. In the all-important annual *Down Beat* poll, the Harry James Orchestra struggled to make Number 12 in the Swing Band list.

In the months that followed Sinatra returned to the studio for another four sessions. Among the songs recorded was the Altman/Lawrence number "All or Nothing at All". At the time, it made little impact, selling only 8,000 copies. Rereleased four years later, the single became an immediate bestseller.

CHAPTER TWO

FLYING SOLO, 1939

The following Christmas, 1939, Sinatra found himself in Chicago. All the top bands were in town to play a Christmas benefit sponsored by the mayor, and it was here that Sinatra was summoned to call on bandleader Tommy Dorsey at his hotel. Sinatra knew why and he knew what his answer was before the question left Dorsey's lips. It was well known in music circles that Tommy Dorsey's vocalist Jack Leonard was thinking about leaving the band to go solo.

The Tommy Dorsey band was a significant step up for Sinatra. It was established and respected. Frank would no longer have to suffer the indignities experienced with Harry James — they had recently been thrown out of a nightclub in mid-song when it was decided they were too brash for the low-key venue. Dorsey was the big time. "He was like a god," said Sinatra. "We were all in awe of him in the music business." As it happened, Dorsey was almost as impressed with Sinatra. Although an earlier audition had gone terribly wrong when Sinatra, overawed by the situation, had lost his voice, Dorsey had since been impressed with a demo copy of "All or Nothing at All" sent to him by Hank Sanciola. But the real turning point came when he heard Sinatra accompany James in the Panther Room of the Sherman Hotel, Chicago, that Christmas. "My back was to the bandstand, but when the kid started taking a chorus, I had to turn around," said Dorsey. "I couldn't resist going back the next night to hear him again."

Sinatra was still under contract to James, which could have been a problem, but James generously tore up the contract and released the young singer. "Nancy was expecting a baby," he said, "and Frank needed the money. I wasn't going to stand in his way." Future splits would not always be so civilized.

"I'm going to the top," Sinatra warned sweetheart Nancy Barbato, "and I don't want anyone dragging on my neck". Nancy got the message, and they married in 1939.

By January 1940, Sinatra was stepping on to the stage in Rockford, Illinois, with a new line-up. The years to come with Dorsey's band were in many ways the most significant in his career.

Arranger Axel Stordahl was one of the first to stretch out a friendly hand to Sinatra, beginning a musical collaboration that would last for many years. Unlike James's band, in which the singer was just about tolerated, Dorsey's was positively geared towards vocals: vocalist Connie Haines arrived with Sinatra and the quartet the Pied Pipers were already well established. Stordahl was primarily a vocalist's arranger, so for the first time Sinatra had someone batting for him.

Nevertheless, the early months weren't easy. Former vocalist Jack Leonard had been very popular, particularly with some members of the band who, according to Sinatra, "resented a newcomer in his place." Sinatra and drummer Buddy Rich apparently came to blows on more than one occasion and Sinatra's competitive behaviour towards Connie Haines left most of the musicians sympathizing with her. An early picture of the band speaks volumes: everyone is smiling but Frank. His face is filled with barely disguised frustration. He is part of a highly successful team, but the truth is written all over his thin features — he wants to be out front, alone, not part of anybody's line-up.

Trombonist and bandleader Tommy Dorsey became a mentor to Sinatra after he joined the band in 1940.

One of the boys. Sinatra pictured with Dorsey (centre), drummer Buddy Rich, trumpeter Ziggy Elman and head of Columbia Records Manie Sachs (third, second and extreme right), as they watch a screening of their first film, 'Las Vegas Nights'.

Some of the resentment towards Sinatra can be explained by the speed with which he became popular with the public. He also established a special relationship with Dorsey, who became something of a father figure. Sinatra's admiration for Dorsey extended to emulating his lifestyle, but began with Dorsey's musical style, elements of which Sinatra transferred to his vocals. "I never took my eyes off his back," he said. "He'd stand there playing his trombone and I'd swear the son of a bitch wasn't breathing. I couldn't even see his jacket move —nothing." It later transpired that Dorsey was well aware of the singer's fascination with his breathing technique, but bided his time before putting him out of his misery. "He explained to me how he would sneak short breaths out of the corners of his mouth at certain points in the arrangement," Sinatra later recalled. "I do the same thing in a song."

There is endless mythology attached to the Sinatra style and technique, in particular his unusual and often extended phrasing, and his expressive focus on the lyric. Sinatra apparently tried everything from underwater swimming to distance running in order to perfect his breathing. Having learned initially from Dorsey's trombone skills, he then looked elsewhere for clues. "I studied the violin playing of Heifetz to see how he moved his bow over the fiddle and back again without seeming to pause, and applied it to singing." Dorsey's second tip was that Frank should listen to Crosby: "All that matters to him is the words." Sinatra had been a fan of Bing since his late teens but he

Sinatra in
his element at a
1940s recording
session alongside
influential collaborator
Axel Stordahl.

"After eight bars I was
thinking 'This is the
greatest sound I've ever
heard,' " said harmony
vocalist Jo Stafford (the
only female in the
group) of Sinatra's first
performance with the
band. By the time this
picture was taken
Sinatra was on the
brink of leaving to start
his solo career, and the
honeymoon years with
Nancy were drawing to
a close.

knew his worst mistake would be to join the ranks of his imitators. "It occurred to me that maybe the world didn't need another Crosby," Sinatra told *Life* magazine many years later. "I decided to experiment a little . . . What I finally hit on was more the Italian *Bel canto* style of singing, without making a point of it." (*Bel canto* is characterized by beauty of tone rather than dramatic power.)

With practice Sinatra learned to incorporate into his vocals the *legato* phrasing and expertly executed *glissandi* he so much admired in Dorsey's trombone solos. He mastered the Dorsey technique of holding a note, drawing air through the corner of his mouth without interrupting the flow. In turn, this newfound ability to sing long, unbroken phrases allowed him to draw attention to the lyric by placing emphasis on key words and phrases. He also learned how to use the microphone to maximum effect. "I use all the colour changes I can get into my voice," he said. "The microphone catches the softest tone, a whisper. I sing love songs and I mean them." The overall effect is such that it is almost impossible not to listen to the lyric when Sinatra is at his best. He is concerned with telling an emotional story and bringing the listener with him, something made possible by a technique learned in those early Dorsey days.

Constant touring meant Sinatra's life took place in a series of hotel rooms and as an up-and-coming musician, he found that women were one of life's perks. For once, Sinatra's timing was off the mark:

he had married too young. His blossoming career left little room for Nancy, and things could only grow worse with the birth of their first child, also named Nancy, in June 1940. Nancy Senior was well aware of her husband's infidelity, but she loved him and, believing, against substanstial evidence to the contrary, that she was the one he would return to in the end, she tolerated it for many, many years.

The initial response to Dorsey's latest discovery was lukewarm. One of Sinatra's early recordings with the band, "I'll Never Smile Again", reached Number 1, but still he was just another band vocalist, only Number 22 in the all-important *Billboard* poll of male vocalists. "Sinatra," the magazine wrote that May, "a good ballad singer, is nil on showmanship." But the constant exposure he received with the band paid off in other areas. His first movie part was in *Las Vegas Nights*, a lightweight story of showgirls and casinos described as "dull" and "laboured" by the *New York Times*. In his second film, though, *Ship Ahoy*, Sinatra and the band were more integral to the fairly ludicrous plot (which climaxes with star Eleanor Powell exposing foreign agents by tap dancing out a message in morse code). This time Sinatra had two numbers and was singled out in reviews.

Gradually Sinatra's voice became a familiar radio favourite. Things started to pick up speed and by the end of the year, aged twenty-five, he was named *Billboard's* top band vocalist. A year later

During his years with Dorsey Sinatra made his first two feature film appearances, in 'Las Vegas Nights' (left) and 'Ship Ahoy' (above right). "It was a wonderful life," he said later. "They were great days".

In 1943 Sinatra was sneered at by critics when he played a series of concerts with the country's leading philharmonic orchestras. Masterminded by publicist George Evans, the concerts were a popular success and financially benefitted the orchestras.

he knocked his one-time idol, Bing Crosby, from his position at the top of the *Down Beat* poll, where Crosby had reigned supreme since the mid Thirties. Suddenly, Sinatra was bigger than the band. It was time for his solo career to take off.

Tommy Dorsey was no fool. Not only did he realize that Sinatra's voice was too good to remain hidden within a band set-up, he had also seen the effect Sinatra had on an audience. "I used to stand there on the bandstand so amazed I'd almost forget to take my solos," he said. "You could almost feel the excitement coming up out of the crowds when that kid stood up to sing. Remember, he was no matinee idol. He was a skinny kid with big ears. And yet what he did to women was something awful."

In the Forties, attention focused heavily on Sinatra's appeal to his female audience, but in time his attraction proved far broader. Sinatra is that rare beast, both a man's man and a ladies' man. Today the same kind of macho charm can be seen in actors like Jack Nicholson, Clint Eastwood and Robert de Niro. Then, it could be said of Marlon Brando and to a lesser extent Dean Martin. When Sinatra was asked by Victor Records to make some solo recordings, Dorsey didn't bother to protest. He may not have liked it, but he knew he couldn't stop it. Sinatra had "star potential" and Dorsey knew when he was beaten.

"The hottest thing in showbiz," said Variety of the new solo Sinatra. **"The proclamation of a new era,"** trumpeted 'Life' magazine, referring to the rise of the soloist and the fall of the big band.

When Sinatra left Dorsey he enraged the bandleader by poaching arranger Axel Stordahl.

On 19 January 1942, Frank Sinatra was where he wanted to be. With Axel Stordahl at the helm, he recorded "Night and Day", "The Night We Called It a Day", "The Song is You" and "Lamplighter's Serenade". Stordahl was with Sinatra when he heard the advance dubs for the first time in a hotel room at the Hollywood Plaza. They spent the afternoon together, playing and replaying the two sides. "Frank just couldn't believe his ears," Stordahl later recalled. "He was so excited, you almost believed he had never recorded before. I think this was a turning point in his career . . . he began to see what he might do on his own."

As far as Sinatra was concerned he had known all along. The only thing that had been holding him up was convincing others. That same day, he told lyricist Sammy Cahn that he was leaving Dorsey. His self-belief, especially for a first-timer, made quite an impression on Victor's A and R man, Harry Meyerson, who supervised the recording session. "Frank was not like a band vocalist at all. He came in self-assured, slugging. He knew exactly what he wanted. Most singers tend to begin with the humble bit. At first they're licking your hand. Then the moment they catch a big one you can't get them on the phone." Sinatra was clearly different, he says. "Popularity didn't really change Sinatra. He started out by having a good opinion of himself. On that first date, he stood his ground and displayed no humility, phoney or real."

Going solo was a calculated risk for Sinatra. He would immediately lose the security he had with Dorsey: the name, the reputation, the top-class bookings. He had seen others like Jack Leonard try and fail. On the other hand he knew Stordahl had faith in him and was aware that Manie Sachs at Columbia was vaguely interested in signing him.

It was bound to be an emotional business. Dorsey always took it personally when someone left, and he and Sinatra had more than a straight business relationship (they were so close that Dorsey became godfather to Sinatra's first child). To make matters worse, Sinatra wanted to take Stordahl with him. Stordahl had been with Dorsey for seven years and was reluctant to take the leap, but, like his mother before him, Sinatra wouldn't take no for an answer. When he offered Stordahl five times what he was earning with Dorsey, Stordahl went.

Dorsey, wounded but mad, drove a hard bargain. He released Frank and even forwarded him the $17,000 advance he needed to set himself up. (Although Sinatra had been on a good wage with Dorsey he never saved a penny.) In return Dorsey wanted a third of Sinatra's gross earnings over $100 a week for the next ten years. Another ten per cent commission was to go to Dorsey's manager for introducing Sinatra to Columbia. Sinatra signed. He saved his regret for later, rather grandly slipping into the third person to tell the *New*

"The boy in every corner drugstore", says Sinatra of his teen appeal.

Sinatra built on his early radio career with "Your Hit Parade".

Overleaf: Meanwhile, the kids went wild at the Paramount. "Sinatra has the ability to believe implicitly the rythmic goo he sings," wrote George Frazire for 'Life' in 1943. "He is utterly convinced that a kiss is still a kiss, a sigh still a sigh."

York Herald Tribune, "You can quote Sinatra as saying he believes it is wrong for anybody to own a piece of him and collect on it when that owner is doing nothing for Sinatra." Although it sounds like a terrible deal, it wasn't so bad in its day – Dean Martin managed to sell over 100 per cent of himself at the start of his career. When MCA signed Sinatra the following year, they renegotiated to pay Dorsey off, and the break was complete.

Sinatra's break with Dorsey was significant in more ways than one; it marked the beginning of the Mafia rumours which were to dog Sinatra throughout his career. Accounts differ wildly, but a strong rumour began to circulate that Dorsey had only agreed to end the contract when leaned on by New Jersey Mobster Willie Moretti. At the time, this was vehemently denied by all concerned. Despite Sinatra's growing reputation for socializing with men connected with the Mob, it was seen by many as no more than colourful copy. The issue became cloudier ten years later, when Dorsey gave an interview in which he admitted he had been visited by heavies and given a violent ultimatum that forced his hand. He may have been speaking the truth after what he considered to be a safe waiting period. On the other hand, he may have been justifying a business decision which, with hindsight, no one but a fool would have made willingly. (He was paid $60,000 to give up thirty-three per cent of a man who went on to earn an estimated $4 million between 1944 and 1946.)

In 1942 Sinatra made another brief appearance in a forgettable film, *Reveille with Beverley*, but things started to look up when Manie Sachs set him up with a CBS radio show, *Songs by Sinatra*. The exposure led to bookings and one of these attracted Bob Weitman, manager of the New York Paramount Theatre. Like Dorsey, he was stunned by the effect Sinatra had on his female audience. "As soon as they saw him the kids went crazy. And when he started to sing, they stood up and yelled and moaned and carried on until I thought, you should excuse the expression, his pants had fallen down." Weitman was in the process of putting together a big Christmas show. The headliner was clarinettist and bandleader Benny Goodman, who had never heard of Sinatra but agreed to take him as an "extra added attraction".

When Sinatra stepped on to the stage of the Paramount that Christmas, Goodman experienced the "trousers down" effect for himself. "The kids let out the loudest scream you ever heard," Sinatra told journalist and biographer Robin Douglas-Home. "Goodman had never heard the kids holler before and he froze – with his arms raised on the up beat. He looked round over one shoulder and said, to no one in particular, "What the fuck was that?"

Sinatra was a hit. The Paramount was packed for the four-week run with Goodman, after which Sinatra went on to fill the theatre for

The cameras were never far away. "Frank Sinatra relaxing in Paramount dressing room amid wardrobe," read this press release.

Queues for Sinatra's performances broke records as Swoonatrics converged on the Paramount Theatre, New York.

a further four weeks without him. Extra security was brought in to handle the fans and the press seized on the story. "Not since the days of Rudolph Valentino has American womanhood made such unabashed public love to an entertainer," screamed *Time* magazine.

It was around this time that Sinatra teamed up with top PR man George Evans. Evans is sometimes credited with single-handedly creating what soon became known as the bobbysoxer phenomenon. At forty, he was extremely good at his job, but he was less a creator than an ace manipulator. When he saw the Sinatra phenomenon in action he knew exactly how to make the most of it. He had boundless energy and enthusiasm and there are endless entertaining tales of the publicity stunts he orchestrated to cash in on his new client's appeal. He is said to have hired squads of carefully briefed teenagers instructed to cry and pass out on cue and laid on first-aid teams armed with ammonia to treat the armies of swooners. Whatever he did, he made sure the press had advance notice and virtually wrote their copy for them, creating a buzz word or nickname for every headline. Sinatra became Swoonatra, his fans Sinatratics. With Evans's encouragement, fan clubs flourished: The Flatbush Girls Who Would Lay Down Their Lives For Frank Sinatra and The Sighing Society Of Sinatra Swooners. There were fan meetings, swooning contests, fanzines, interviews — all adding up to unending publicity. It came as no surprise to those in the industry when Evans was rewarded with a special *Billboard* award in 1943 for the Most Effective Promotion of a Single Personality.

Unusually for a man used to taking control, Sinatra was now being swept along by events. Talking about this phase in his life many years later he described a phenomenon many here-today-gone-tomorrow pop sensations have since struggled to put into words. "I was — I was everything. Happy? I don't know. I wasn't unhappy, let's put it that way. I never had it so good. Sometimes I wonder whether anybody ever had it like that, before or since. It was the darndest thing, wasn't it? But I was too busy ever to know whether I was happy, or even to ask myself. I can't remember for a long time even taking time out to think."

Bobbysoxer madness peaked with the legendary Paramount show, dubbed the Columbus Day Riot. Traffic was brought to a standstill as over 20,000 bobbysoxers stormed Times Square trying to join a queue six deep, ticket booths were smashed and bystanders trampled underfoot. Today's celebrity-watchers have become blasé about the excesses of teen adulation, but in 1943 it still needed explaining.

Singer Connie Haines, who watched Sinatra develop, offered one explanation: "It was something about him being so frail and skinny. Something about the way he'd hang on to that microphone. Something in his singing that reached out to his audience — like he was saying, I'm giving this to you with everything I got; what have you got to give me?" An entry to a radio competition — "Why I Like Sinatra" — reprinted in the highbrow *New Yorker* as part of a piece by E.J. Kahn suggests Haines got it right: "I think he is one of the greatest things that ever happened to teenage America," wrote the devoted bobbysoxer. "We were kids that never got much attention, but he's made us feel like we are something. He has given us understanding. Something we need. Most adults don't think we need any consideration. We're really human and Frank realizes that." Long before Elvis, Sinatra was the first pop star to identify music with teenage independence and identity.

The most popular theory was hysteria brought about by the war — with young men away, young women were pining; with fathers away, teenage degeneracy was rampant. Psychologists had a field day: did the childlike figure gripping the microphone engender

"I used to bring binoculars," wrote Martha Weinman Lear in the 'New York Times' of her early years as a fan, **"just to watch the lower lip. And then, the other thing: the voice had that trick, that funny little sliding, skimming slur that it would do coming off the end of a note. It drove us bonkers . . . it was an invitation to hysteria . . . we'd start swooning all over the place, in the aisles, on each other's shoulders, in the arms of cops. Whatever he stirred beneath our barely budding breasts, it wasn't motherly."**

Sinatra the father, seen decorating his home in Hasbrouck Heights with daughter Nancy, aged three.

Family shots were usually stage managed by George Evans, seen with Sinatra and Alec Wilder (right), as Sinatra conducts the Wilder Program, a brave move for a man who couldn't read music.

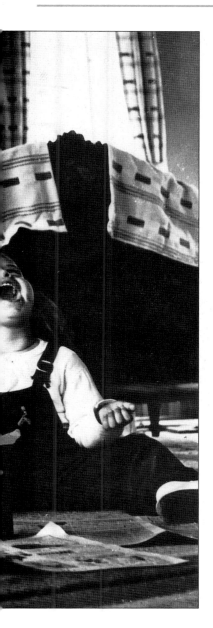

maternal instincts? Was "music-induced swooning" psychologically harmful? The moral majority found him guilty of corrupting the nation's youth, branding his music "an opium of emotionalism". His voice was described by one critic as "vocal fondling". But although girls were known to send their bras and panties to the stage for autographing, the most obvious explanation — that teenage girls experienced the same sexual confusion and excitement as boys — was considered utterly beyond the pale. Overt female sexuality was not something the public was ready for and instead Evans wisely built on the notion of Sinatra's boy-next-door appeal.

What Evans presented to the eager public was no less than the American Dream. He showed them Frank the family man wallowing in domestic bliss. By his side, loyal and loving big Nancy and adorable little Nancy. Photoshoots were often done at home to capitalize on this boyish and unthreatening image. No one was to know that Sinatra saw less of his own home than most reporters. Evans had his work cut out. Sinatra's background was a minefield. There was his own arrest for adultery, his Uncle Babe's conviction as accomplice to murder and his mother's arrests for illegal abortions. The present wasn't much better. Sinatra's appetite for women was well known, as was his penchant for gangsters, drinking and boxing. With barefaced cheek even by PR standards Evans rewrote Frank's brief life history. The bored drop-out became a track star who went on to become a sports reporter, Dolly became a Red Cross nurse and the romantic myth of the dirt-poor street kid who fought his way out of the gutter was born.

Yet again Sinatra had found an older mentor. Evans, the father figure, became a part of his life, making friends with Nancy, trying to mend their damaged relationship and constantly covering Sinatra's tracks when he got into trouble. In time, he even took Sinatra's education in hand and set about guiding him politically.

By this time Sinatra was a busy man. He was a regular guest on America's favourite radio shows and had his own spot on *Your Hit Parade*, the country's top networked chart show which doubled its audience within months of his arrival. He also signed a movie deal with RKO.

As many teen idols have since learned to their cost, adoring teenagers make fickle lovers. More importantly, teen idols tend not to be taken seriously as musicians, which leaves them at a loose end once they've outgrown the teen market or the teen market has outgrown them. This was particularly galling to Sinatra, who took himself extremely seriously. As his career progressed he often claimed he was not been given the respect he deserved. He took it very badly, for instance, when he was ridiculed by purists for appearing in concert with America's leading symphony orchestras later that year. His move

Rubbing shoulders with the stars. Sinatra with Jimmy "Schnozzle" Durante.

Arranger Axel Stordahl's distinctive strings were the sound of Sinatra in the mid-forties.

to conquer the nightclub scene at the height of his bobbysoxer period may have been an attempt to pre-empt these problems. If so, his worries were initially confirmed when most nightclubs turned him down as not sufficiently sophisticated. For Sinatra, a man plagued by insecurity, this was like a red rag to a bull and he became determined to crack the clubs. Fortunately it was a boom time for nightlife. The tensions of the war years made live entertainment a popular diversion and even if people were short of money, they were prepared to spend what they had.

In April 1943, the Riobamba took him on at the bottom of the bill for a fraction of the money he was paid for his radio performances. Within a week it was standing room only and Sinatra had star billing. When Walter O'Keefe, who had originally headed the bill, came on for his final show he announced magnanimously, "Ladies and gentlemen, I was your star of the evening, but, tonight, in this club, we have all just seen a star born." Sinatra spent his first ten years being discovered and rediscovered. As far as he was concerned, his success was no more than he had always expected and he rarely missed the opportunity to say so. From the beginning the public caught glimpses of an arrogant, slightly bitter Sinatra, completely at odds with his sensitive and vulnerable stage persona.

By the end of the summer it looked as if there was no stopping him. He dominated the charts with "All or Nothing at All", "You'll Never Know", "People Will Say We're in Love" and "Sunday, Monday or Always". As a live performer he was also in great demand, with the legendary Copacabana and the exclusive Wedgwood Room at the Waldorf competing for his presence. It was particularly important to Sinatra to win over the audience at the Waldorf, which represented precisely the notion of class to which he aspired but of which he would never really be a part – not, as he often supposed, because of his lack of education, but because of the coverage given to his underworld connections and his uncontrollable temper. Although the audience at the Waldorf were prepared to dismiss Sinatra as a dilettante, they couldn't fail to be impressed. "I've always dreamed of working at the Waldorf-Astoria," Frank told his appreciative audience at the end of his show, "it's sort of the tops."

Demand grew, his price went up and no gossip column was complete without a mention of Sinatra's name. At the same time a combination of the pressure and the glory brought out the worst excesses of the Sinatra personality. As he had always done, he built a close group of insiders around him. Later it would be the Rat Pack, then the Clan, this time it was the Varsity. The select group included long-time sidekicks Sanciola and Sevano as well as the ever-patient Axel Stordahl. Songwriter Jimmy Van Heusen was also one of the inner circle, as were Sammy Cahn, Manie Sachs, his business partner Ben Barton and a couple of heavies, boxers Tami Mauriello (in whom Sinatra had bought a stake in 1943) and Al Silvani. Those close to him grew accustomed to tiptoeing around his fragile ego and swallowing their pride in the face of his violent and unpredictable outbursts. It was that or enter into a lifetime feud. Sinatra was never able to forgive and forget; once riled he could be mercilessly cruel. Behind the scenes he was allegedly referred to as "the monster" and George Evans as "Frankenstein".

The Varsity became a regular fixture at the Madison Square Garden Friday night fights. Then as now, fights were about atmosphere, with the crowds they attracted as much a part of the action as the fights themselves. Like the nightclub scene, it was a place where the entertainment world and the underworld overlapped. It was a highly macho exercise run along lines Sinatra understood. The rules of the fight game leave no room for grey areas. All is black or white. The fighter is alone and alone he wins or loses. This is the way Sinatra experienced the world and the way he responded to it.

Sinatra made a habit of crediting the invisible players, like songwriter Jimmy Van Heusen, co-writer with Sammy Cahn of "All the Way", "My Kind of Town", "September of My Years", "Come Fly With Me" and many others.

CHAPTER THREE

THE SLIPPERY SLOPE: MOVIES, McCARTHYISM AND THE MOB, 1944

Sinatra was first teamed with Gene Kelly for 'Anchors Aweigh' in 1945. Although the new boy on the lot, he threatened to quit unless Jules Styne and Sammy Cahn were taken on to write his songs.

By the time Sinatra arrived in Hollywood to begin his screen career, his name was known from coast to coast. Again, through a combination of luck and judgement, he had timed things just right. His first real acting part was in *Higher and Higher*, a Rodgers and Hart musical given a Hollywood make-over.

The film was nothing special. Most reviewers assumed Sinatra was playing himself although the *New Yorker*, while slating the film, said simply, "Mr Sinatra comes out fine. He has some acting to do, and he does it." Certainly the role did not stretch Sinatra, but demanding parts were not a feature of movie musicals. At the very least he proved he could do more than sing.

His next film was in the same vein, but this time he took the lead. *Step Lively*, a remake of the Marx Brothers' *Room Service*, had been adapted to showcase Frank's talents with songs written for him by Jule Steyn and Sammy Cahn. Cast as a struggling playwright who discovers his voice is his fortune, he was again called upon to play himself, or at least his public self. Sinatra is good enough, but it was standard fare and the reviews said as much. There was also a sign of things to come when Sinatra walked off set over a minor disagreement. His patience and involvement were reserved for music and on only his fifth film he demonstrated his frustration with the process of film-making.

While Sinatra was building his film career on the west coast, Nancy was coping with motherhood in the east. She had been pregnant when Sinatra left for Hollywood and in January 1944 she gave birth to their second child, Frank Jr. Sinatra was busy filming *Step Lively* and missed the birth, just as he had missed the first one. Evans stayed behind to orchestrate the press. If the nightclub circuit had offered Sinatra opportunities to stray, extramarital affairs were

the very lifeblood of Hollywood. Evans did his best, but the press became increasingly judgemental.

There was also growing resentment towards Sinatra for his failure to join up and fight for his country. Other public figures and fellow musicians — Buddy Rich, Ziggy Ellman — were by now in the forces. Sinatra was not only still at home but with his teen adulation supposedly based on the dearth of young men, he was seen by some to be benefiting from the situation. In 1943 he failed the pre-draft medical. An eardrum punctured during his difficult birth meant a 4F classification — unfit for duty. But when, two years later, he was reclassified as 2F, meaning the job he was doing at home was "essential to the national health, safety and interest", the press were moved to ridicule and asked why outstanding athletes and artists were being given special status. Without explanation Sinatra was quickly reclassified as a 4F, but bad feeling remained.

When Sinatra finally did go overseas to entertain the troops it was after VE Day and to the relative safety of Europe and North Africa. Columnist Lee Mortimer wrote, "The 4F from Hasbrouck Heights waited until hostilities were over in the Mediterranean to take his seven-week joy-ride, while fragile dolls like Carole Landis and ageing, ailing men like Joe E. Brown and Al Jolson subjected themselves to enemy action, jungle disease and the dangers of travel through hostile skies from the beginning of the war." Although Mortimer's attack was motivated by a personal grudge against Sinatra, he said what many people were thinking.

THE SLIPPERY SLOPE, 1944

With his film career growing in importance, Frank decided the time had come to move to Hollywood, bringing Nancy and the children with him. It can't have been easy for Nancy to adjust to her husband's fame. While Sinatra was surrounded by gofers, advisors and role models such as Tommy Dorsey and Gene Kelly, Nancy was on her own. Hollywood was like another planet. For support, she took her five married sisters with her, moving one in as her secretary.

Within months of the move Sinatra received the ultimate accolade — an invitation to tea at the White House. The association between celebrities and politicians has a strong tradition in America. While Crosby aligned himself with the Republicans, Sinatra publicly pledged his vote to the Democrat President, Franklin Roosevelt (after whom he had named his son). He had never lost touch with his mother's political activities, appearing at Democrat rallies when he could. Roosevelt, keen to win the Italian-American vote, welcomed Sinatra on board.

Sinatra's relationship with politics was never easy. Politicians had much to gain by cultivating the relationship but also much to lose. This time around Roosevelt met with press criticism for entertaining a 4F. Worse, Sinatra was a loose cannon. On the night Roosevelt won a fourth term in office, Sinatra was involved in a juvenile row with powerful Republican columnist, Westbrook Pegler. Each claimed to have been taunted by the other, resulting in Sinatra refusing to play the Wedgwood Room while Pegler was in the audience. Pegler retaliated by printing an article exposing Sinatra's 1938 morals charge.

Publicity stills of Sinatra with recruits in California, and touring service camps, could not disguise the fact that Sinatra's military involvment was minimal.

He did become politically involved at home, actively supporting Franklin D. Roosevelt with Dorsey and the First Lady, and with Ethel Merman in campaigning spirit.

Jules Styne (left) and
Jimmy Van Heusen
(right) both worked
with songwriter Sammy
Cahn at different times,
providing Sinatra with
a string of Oscar
winning numbers.

In late 1944 Sinatra started recording again in earnest. He was still working with Stordahl and being fed wonderful material by Sammy Cahn and Jules Styne, plus the occasional number by Cole Porter or Jimmy Van Heusen. His two chart successes were "Saturday Night is the Loneliest Night of the Week" and "I Dream of You". He also began to experiment with new types of music, recording a number of gospel songs with a black gospel group, the Charioteers, and some Latin numbers with Cuban bandleader Xavier Cugat. He even tried his hand at conducting a composition by Alec Wilder with a full orchestra. A brave move for a man who couldn't read music. "If I learned . . ." he once said, "it would probably louse up my feelings."

In 1945, Sinatra was still taking flak for his war record. In an attempt to make amends George Evans decided to make the most of Frank's relationship with teenage America. Sinatra began to visit schools and youth centres, lecturing on the need for education and the dangers of racial discrimination and delinquency. He may not have been the slum kid his publicity profile suggested, but he knew what it was like to be called a dago and had genuinely strong views on racism. He also knew what might have happened to an uneducated kid like himself without his particular talent.

Sinatra made two films in 1945 and they couldn't have been more different. One was his biggest box office to date, the other

unexpectedly delivered his first Academy Award. RKO had been riding the Sinatra wave, happily cashing in but unsure how to develop him as a screen performer in a way that would outlast his teen appeal. It took another studio to realize that the swooning had to stop and that the smart move was to anticipate this by giving Sinatra more to do. His contract allowed him to make one picture a year outside RKO, and MGM's *Anchors Aweigh* (1945) was the one to offer him the escape he needed.

Anchors Aweigh teamed Sinatra with the more experienced Gene Kelly in parts which reflected their off-screen relationship. The film tells the story of two sailors on shore leave: Joe (Kelly) is the wisecracking Don Juan and Clarence (Sinatra) the shy, inexperienced geek who tags along to learn from the master. The big production numbers in blinding technicolor are the main feature of the film, the crowd-pleasers, especially the ground-breaking routine in which live action combines with animation to allow Kelly to dance with Jerry the mouse. It's Kelly's film and he choreographed the big dance numbers, but Sinatra, a natural mover, holds his own with apparent ease. The dialogue, littered with Gees and Gollys, is often cloying and Sinatra sometimes overdoes the vulnerable bit — smiling dumbly a little too often and batting his eyelashes a little too ferociously — but the overall exuberance of the film wins out. The *New York Times* called it "a humdinger of a musical". It was the film that put Kelly on the map, but also established Sinatra as a competent all-rounder.

While stories of Sinatra's early career as a sports writer were no more than PR mythology, his interest in fighting racism was genuine and longstanding. He lectured in schools, and in the same year he made 'Anchors Aweigh', received a special Academy Award for the anti-racist short film, 'The House That I Live In'.

The House I Live In, made the same year, is a ten-minute RKO short from an original screenplay by Albert Maltz, a card-carrying communist who later found himself blacklisted and at the centre of a row between Sinatra, the press and the Kennedys. It was an extremely worthy project aimed at confronting racial and religious intolerance by using Sinatra as a figure to whom kids on the street could relate. Those involved gave their services free, profits went to organizations fighting juvenile deliquency and the film won a special Academy Award. It raised Sinatra's profile as a celebrity liberal and also raised the hackles of the Republican press with whom Sinatra was to begin a long running battle.

In the film Sinatra plays himself. In a break from rehearsals at the recording studio, he slips into the back alley for a breath of air and catches a group of boys bullying another boy — "because we don't like his religion". Sinatra talks to them about racism, in a language they understand, then turns to go back to work. "Hey," shouts one of the kids, "what do you do for a living?" "I sing," says Sinatra. "Aw, you're kidding," says another. "No," replies Sinatra, "I'll show you" and moves into the title song.

Sinatra's personal experience and emotional conviction made him a natural communicator on racism. And Evans, the committed liberal and dedicated PR, did all he could to develop Sinatra's social leanings as a counterbalance to his rocky marriage, poor war record and Mob associations. Through Evans Sinatra met and was influenced by other socialists. He was also pointed in the direction of left-wing authors and politicians, a natural progression from his mother's political work. The reputation that grew from his involvement led to Sinatra's attempt to end a strike in Gary, Indiana, in which white high-school students were refusing to share classrooms with black classmates, and later to his appearance before the House UnAmerican Activities Committee.

Initially his political involvement was rewarded with a string of commendations and awards from organizations fighting intolerance — the Bureau of Intercultural Education, the National Conference of Christians and Jews, the New Jersey Organization of Teachers, and others. No one could have known how nasty things were about to become as HUAC cranked into gear. Sinatra was one of the first targets.

Anti-communist feelings had been running high since the end of the war. There was pressure on the film industry to present the American Way as the only way forward and films like *The House I Live In* which showed a less than perfect vision of America, were met with criticism from the dominant right-wing press and politicians. At a time when paranoia was rife, influential figures like Sinatra were seen as a danger to national security. With the support of the right-wing

Sinatra pictured with the doyenne of the gossip columnists, Louella Parsons, and with singer Lena Horne.

Sinatra and Nancy pictured at a premiere in 1946 – publicly united but privately at odds.

At his peak everyone was happy to associate themselves with Sinatra the star.

Motion Picture Alliance for the Preservation of American Ideals, Republican Congressman J. Parnell Thomas (later jailed for fraud) set to work identifying subversive individuals and films. Once identified, often by colleagues acting as co-operative witnesses, they were called to trial. "Are you now or have you ever been a member of the communist party?" they were asked. Some refused to answer, taking shelter behind the First Amendment which asserts the right to freedom of belief, but many saw their careers and lives ruined. Sinatra initially dealt with accusations lightheartedly — "Somebody said I spoke like a communist," he told the *Daily Worker*. "You know they call Shirley Temple a communist too. Well, me and Shirley both, I guess" — but was eventually pressured into publicly denouncing communism. This didn't stop headlines such as "Red Scare Sinatra" and "Sinatra Faces Probe on Red Ties" contributing to the flurry of bad publicity that changed the course of his career in 1947.

The American national press was dominated by the right-wing Hearst and Scripps-Howard publishing empires and once they got their hooks in they went to town on other "unAmerican" aspects of Sinatra's character — the volatile temper, the undemocratic behaviour he demonstrated in his personal life, the underworld connections. According to many commentators, powerful journalists from Hearst and Scripps-Howard never forgave Sinatra his early liberalism and continued to wage war against him over the decades, making a significant impact on the public image still with him today. Unfortunately, Sinatra supplied them with plenty of ammunition.

In the mid Forties Sinatra's position seemed unassailable. He had established his screen potential and was voted Most Popular Film Star by *Modern Screen* magazine. He had shown the music world he was more than just a teen idol (and still received over 5,000 fan letters a week) and he was in the middle of some of his busiest years as a performer and recording artist. In 1946–47 he recorded over 120 songs, including "The Coffee Song" and "Five Minutes More", both hits. He also won *Down Beat's* award for the country's favourite singer for the third consecutive year and took *Metronome's* award for best male vocalist. He even won his Academy Award basically for being a nice guy.

But there were rumours. And rumours spawned stories, features, headlines and eventually a fall from grace for a man who only knew how to move up. His two highly publicized affairs with actresses Marylin Maxwell and Lana Turner were just the tip of the iceberg and Nancy knew it. Now living in the thick of things, she could no longer remain determinedly in the dark. It was a time in Hollywood when an entertainer's private life was considered public property and Nancy's only means of defence was to learn to play the game by Hollywood rules. Private dramas were often played out in

FRANK SINATRA—sensational star of his own radio program, Wednesday nights over CBS.

GENERAL ELECTRIC PRESENTS

the First and Only

SELF-CHARGING PORTABLE RADIO

Here's a new portable that does what no other radio ever did before. It renews its battery power over and over again. It's self-charging.

No Battery Worries

Play it all you please with never a worry about the trouble and expense of regular battery replacements. Until you actually see and hear it you won't believe that any portable can be so smart, so light, so small. And still have such big-set performance—such big-set tone—such big-set power and selectivity.

Play it wherever you go—on picnics—on boats—on trains. Then indoors—just plug it in to AC house current. Even while you play this General Electric self-charging portable like any table set, the compact storage battery recharges for more hours of carefree entertainment anywhere.

Built Like A Battleship

Hear this amazing portable radio at your General Electric dealer's—now. See the beautiful plastic finish—the sturdy aluminum case. Open the back. You'll marvel at masterful engineering such as you never saw before in any radio. Tune in more stations with more power and clearer natural color tone than you get on most large sets. This G-E self-charging portable will be your prized companion—everywhere.

GENERAL ⓖⓔ ELECTRIC
170-ER

LEADER IN RADIO, TELEVISION AND ELECTRONICS

RADIOS

☆ GOOD-BYE BATTERY WORRIES!

☆ NATURAL COLOR TONE

☆ RENEWS ITS POWER OVER AND OVER AGAIN

This tiny leak proof storage battery furnishes full constant power. (All other portables use dry batteries — performance is limited—their power fades rapidly as batteries age.)

Built like a battleship. All vital parts protected in sturdy compartments which also give inherent electronic shielding. The first peace time use of such compact, military design.

public and favoured gossip columnists were used as mouthpieces to make public statements on private matters. Following one of their separations, a public reunion was orchestrated after Sinatra made a guest appearance on Phil Silvers' bill to sing "Going Home". A concerned Silvers then led him to Nancy's table for a public embrace. In the subsequent radio interview he spoke of spending more time at home and building a home in the country for his family. Such theatricals were not unusual amongst celebrities whose private lives were under scrutiny, but Sinatra never liked it and gradually ceased to tolerate it at all.

In 1946 Sinatra joined Bergman, Bogart, Crosby, Hope, Cooper and others at MGM. Impressed with *Anchors Aweigh*, the studio offered him a lucrative contract including the right to make one non-MGM movie each year and the promise that he could continue his radio and recording work. They saw him as a musical star and their first move was to cast him in the disastrous Jerome Kern bio-pic, *Till the Clouds Roll By*, in which Sinatra was one of a long list of stars to perform Kern's well-loved songs. Perched on a white pedestal, dressed in gleaming white tuxedo, shoes, shirt and bow tie, Sinatra sang "Ol' Man River" amidst a sea of white-clad band members. The vocals were praised, but the notion of presenting a black elegy to white exploitation in such a tasteless manner was described by *Life* as the year's worst on-screen moment. Critics used it to attack the authenticity of Sinatra's involvement in *The House I Live In*, which had come out shortly before. Less attention was given to Sinatra's insistence on changing the lyrics from "Darkies all work on the Mississippi" to "Here we all work on the Mississippi".

Next came *It Happened in Brooklyn*. Sinatra was no longer the keen, co-operative, hard-working professional he had been five years before; now he frequently missed rehearsals and left the lot without permission. In his music career, he was used to being in control. But this was the studio system, in which an actor's every move was determined by the studio heads. The same journalists who had attacked his political activities from his support of Roosevelt onwards, were delighted to publicize his personal and career problems.

Finally, there were the Mob rumours which peaked in 1947 with the Lucky Luciano incident. Luciano was believed to have united the various Mafia clans at the end of Prohibition in the 1930s to form a power base known as the Syndicate or the Organization. After being convicted and imprisoned on probition charges he was deported from America but was now calling a summit meeting of Syndicate bosses in preparation for his return. It was essentially a matter of paying respects in the traditional manner. The meeting took place in Havana, Cuba and coincided with a visit by Sinatra, who flew in on the same plane as Rocco and Joe Fischetti, cousins of Al Capone and

Sinatra celebrates New Year with longtime pal Phil Silvers.

Sinatra singing "Ol Man River". "My idea with that song," said writer Jerome Kern, "was to have a rabbity little fellow do it - somebody who made you believe he was tired of livin' and scared of dyin'".

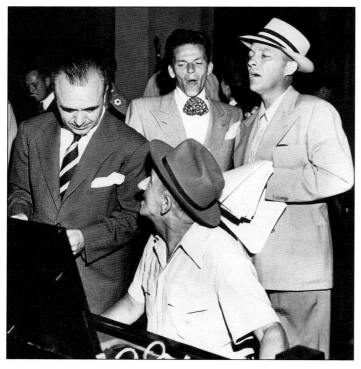

Relaxing between broadcasts with Bing Crosby and Judy Garland, and with Bing, Jose Iturbi and Jimmy Durante during recording for an armed forces radio show in 1945.

Hoboken's most famous son rides into town on a fire engine, accompanied by his father.

leading figures in the Chicago crime family. Sinatra was then accused of spending four days wining, dining and gambling America's most violent criminals. After a tip off from the Federal Narcotics Bureau, who were watching developments very carefully, Scripps-Howard journalist Robert Ruark offered an unnecessarily vitriolic account of Sinatra's meeting with Luciano: "This curious desire to cavort among the scum is possibly permissible among citizens who are not peddling sermons to the nation's youth . . . But Mr Sinatra, self-confessed saviour of the country's small-fry, seems to be setting a most peculiar example for his hordes of pimply, shrieking slaves."

Sinatra claimed rather weakly that a coincidence had brought him to town while the Mob was there. He realized he was laying himself open to criticism by sitting and drinking with them, he said, but found it hard to extricate himself once he had been invited. The story made the headlines. Sinatra's explanation was similar to the one he would serve up regularly throughout his career: "I was brought up to shake a man's hand when I am introduced to him without first investigating his past." In other words, the worlds of entertainers and racketeers frequently overlapped. Sinatra sang in bars, nightclubs and casinos, and men connected with the underworld had financial interests in those establishments. It was inevitable they should have some social contact, and *not* to shake hands, not to have a drink, not to pay your respects to these men would have been extremely foolish for a man in Sinatra's line of work — or indeed any man who valued his health. Dean Martin, Jerry Lewis, Sammy Davis Jr and others have all told stories of being introduced to the big boys. All did what was expected of them. It would have been stupid not to. Sometimes "paying respects" meant flying across the country at the drop of a hat to perform in clubs run by members of the Mob, but that's show business, they said.

There was slightly more to it in Sinatra's case. He was enamoured of these men and certainly didn't discourage social contact. Characters like Willie Moretti and later Sam Giancana were seen with him regularly over a period of years. But whatever Sinatra's motives for sitting down to dinner with criminals, having his picture taken with them or playing golf with them, no concrete criminal link between him and the Mob has ever been proven in court. The likelihood is that a certain amount of backscratching went on, favours were exchanged and rules were bent, but beyond that the role of Sinatra within the Mob may be as much media invention as fact. One of the most ludicrous stories was connected with the Cuba summit meeting, but emerged a few years later when the incident was revived to discredit Sinatra in time for the 1951 election. Lee Mortimer, again using information leaked by the Federal Narcotics Bureau, claimed that Sinatra had carried $2 million in Mob funds to the summit meeting.

"Picture me," said Sinatra incredulously, "skinny Frankie, lifting two million dollars in small bills . . . 1,000 dollars in dollar bills weighs three pounds, which makes the load I was supposed to have carried 6,000 pounds. Even assuming that the bills were twenties — the bag still would have required a few stevedores to carry it." He had a point.

Whatever the extent of Sinatra's involvement, it was certainly a big mistake to believe he could pursue his political aspirations and continue to associate with criminals on *any* level. He was simply too famous and the hypocrisy too visible. He had been targeted by the press, some of whom had developed a very personal dislike of him and were watching his every move. Something had to give.

CHAPTER FOUR

A FOOL TO WANT HER, 1948

It Happened in Brooklyn opened shortly after the Cuba debacle and the smear campaign continued. "This excellent and well produced picture," wrote Lee Mortimer, ". . . bogs down under the miscast Frank (Lucky) Sinatra, smirking and trying to play a leading man." Trouble had been brewing between Sinatra and Mortimer for some time and Sinatra had often threatened to do something about Mortimer's very personalized attacks.

A month later, while dining at Ciro's, a Hollywood nightclub, he spotted Mortimer. Accounts of what happened next vary considerably. Depending on who's telling the story, Mortimer either provoked Sinatra into an attack or Sinatra pursued and punched Mortimer. Either way, Sinatra ended up in Beverly Hills Justice Court on a battery charge. The Hearst organization went to town, hiring a fleet of attorneys to represent their reporter in court and giving the story disproportionately extensive coverage. Facing a possible six-month jail sentence, Sinatra took Louis B. Mayer's advice, settling out of court and apologizing publicly to Mortimer for an unprovoked attack.

When Sinatra failed to sell out a three-week run at the Capitol Theatre, New York that autumn, Mortimer could not conceal his glee: "Broadway whispers this will be Sinatra's last appearance here and that didn't kill my appetite for the family turkey dinner."

At a time when Sinatra could ill afford problems on the career front, reviews of his latest release, *The Miracle of the Bells*, confirmed suspicions that the role had been a mistake. Contrary to advice from colleagues he had insisted on taking the role of Father Paul, a local priest at the heart of an overly sentimental plot. Despite a cast including Lee J. Cobb and Fred MacMurray, the film did not do well. To make matters worse, Sinatra suffered comparisons with Bing Crosby, who had won an Academy Award for his part as a priest in *Going My Way*, a much better film.

MGM allowed him one more chance to escape from type with *The Kissing Bandit*. "Never any great shakes as a comic," wrote *Cue* magazine, "Mr Sinatra is further handicapped by a weak script, silly

Press relations sunk to an all time low when Sinatra finally rose to columnist Lee Mortimer's taunts, and floored him with a punch outside Ciro's nightclub. "He called me a dago," claimed Sinatra, "so I let him have it". The out-of-court settlement cost Sinatra over 20,000 dollars.

dialogue and uncertain direction." It was a bad film and there was no way Sinatra could emerge unscathed. When *The Kissing Bandit* failed, MGM fell back on the well-worn song-and-dance formula that had worked for Sinatra in the past. In 1949 he was twice paired with Kelly in *Take Me Out to the Ballgame* and *On the Town*. Despite a slim plot about a baseball team with a pretty female manager (Esther Williams), *Take Me Out to the Ballgame* did reasonably well as a summer box-office hit. Far more successful, though, was Kelly and Sinatra's next outing, *On the Town,* described by *Sunday Times* critic George Perry as, "unarguably Sinatra's best musical and a landmark in the genre". In a plot with a familiar ring, Kelly, Sinatra and Jules Munshin play three sailors on shore leave in New York: Kelly the confident, experienced leader, Munshin the gormless fall guy and Sinatra the frail, sincere naif (a role he was getting a little old for at thirty-four). All hope to meet a girl and start by pursuing Vera Ellen, whose face Kelly has seen on a poster. The details don't matter, for the film "is so exuberant," said one critic, "that it threatens at moments to bounce right off the screen." *On the Town* was a resounding hit with both critics and public, but it came too late for Sinatra: he was already sinking too fast for a single film success to save him.

The final professional blow came when Manie Sachs resigned from the board of Columbia Records. While Sachs had encouraged and nurtured Sinatra as Columbia's top vocalist, his replacement, Mitch Miller, was keen to make a mark and concentrated on his own discoveries, such as Tony Bennett and Johnny Ray. Miller was undeniably a commercial animal who seemed to lack Sachs's sensitivity and taste but, whatever his faults, he was not responsible for the changes in the music scene which suddenly left Sinatra out of favour. Just as the soloists had supplanted the big bands, the crooners were being replaced by the belters, led by Frankie Laine and Billy Eckstein. At the same time jazz was hijacked by the high-octane magic of bebop, and the teen market, once Sinatra's sole preserve, had its heart stolen by newcomer Johnny Ray. Only a few years before Sinatra had ruled the roost. Now he found himself pushed from the top of the *Down Beat* poll for the first time since 1943.

As a musician before all else, Sinatra was well attuned to changes in musical style. He could see that the lush Stordahl arrangements that had made him famous were no longer fashionable, but could not rush his evolution from crooner to swinger. Stung by a barrage of harsh criticism, Sinatra abandoned his Saturday evening radio slot, *Your Hit Parade*, in 1949, uncomfortable with the songs he was required to sing and the style in which he was expected to sing them. "Alternately dull, pompous and raucous," said *Metronome* of the show. "Frank sings without relaxation and often at tempos that

The landmark musical, 'On The Town', came too late to halt the decline.

Sinatra's days with Columbia were numbered.

'Take Me Out to the Ball Game' co-starring Gene Kelly, Esther Williams and Betty Garrett.

On the set of 'On the Town' with Kelly and Jules Munshin. The film featured groundbreaking sequences shot in New York city, and owed much to co-director Gene Kelly's innovative ideas.

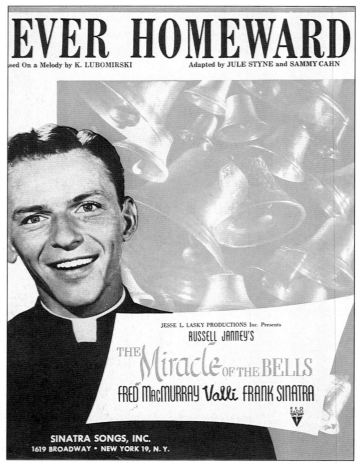

Sinatra often seemed at his most relaxed standing behind a microphone.

While 'It Happened in Brooklyn' fared well, 'The Miracle of the Bells' was a poor choice.

His cinematic ups and downs continued with 'Take Me Out To The Ball Game' scoring well in 1948, and 'The Kissing Bandit' marking a low point the year before.

don't suit him or the songs. Axel [Stordahl] plays murderous, rag-timey junk that he, with his impeccable taste, must abhor . . . Frank sounds worse in these Saturday nightmares than he ever has since he first became famous." When Sinatra's contract expired in 1952, Columbia declined to renew it.

Miller's explanation for Sinatra's slump focused on the singer's private life. "I had nothing to do with him losing his movie contract, losing his television show, losing his radio show," claimed Miller. "His career went down the drain because of his emotional turmoil over Ava Gardner."

Miller had hit the nail on the head. Sinatra's recording and screen careers may already have been in trouble, but the emotional toll exacted by this destructive love affair certainly accelerated the downward slide.

Gardner and Sinatra first met while she was married to Mickey Rooney. He flirted lightheartedly, she was suitably awed. It was the kind of exchange that took place daily between Hollywood stars and hopefuls, nothing extraordinary, and both were married anyway. Somewhere along the line they danced together when Sinatra and Howard Hughes swapped partners at a Palm Springs nightclub. Hughes took to the floor with Sinatra's date, Lana Turner, and Sinatra with Ava. She told a friend that she found him "conceited, arrogant and overpowering"; they didn't see each other for another three years. They later found they were neighbours: he in a busy bachelor pad during one of his periodic separations from Nancy, she in a shared flat next door. They bumped into each other off and on, he asked her out, she went, but nothing came of it. It was after the post-première party for *Gentlemen Prefer Blondes* in early 1949 that sparks began to fly and they began what columnist and biographer Earl Wilson called "a two-year soap opera with screaming fights heard around the world".

The affair quickly took its toll on Sinatra's relationship with the long-suffering Evans, who knew something that Sinatra chose to ignore. For a public already disillusioned with their former idol's alleged Mob connections and all-too-true temper tantrums, the married father of three (his third child, Christina, was born the year before the affair began) parading his affair with Gardner was the final straw. After a series of bitter rows over Sinatra's escapades with Ava, he and Evans fell out, severing a nine-year partnership. With Manie Sachs no longer guiding his music career and Evans no longer looking after his private life, Sinatra was adrift. It was then that Ava became the most important person in his life.

Born on Christmas Eve 1922, Ava Lavinia Gardner was the seventh child of Mary Elizabeth Gardner, herself one of nineteen. She inherited from her mother the green almond eyes, dark hair and

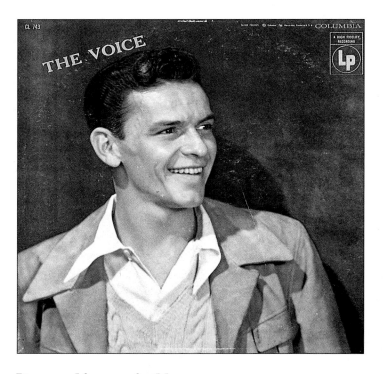

It seemed inconceivable that Columbia should drop their top name.

Happy families: Nancy and Frank with children Nancy and Frank Junior, and youngest daughter Christina. The pictures presented to the public by George Evans were a far from accurate reflection of Sinatra's turbulent personal life. Ava Gardner was the last straw for the long suffering publicist.

Ava had become bandleader Artie Shaw's fourth wife in 1945.

Her relationship with the reclusive millionaire Howard Hughes lasted twenty years, but was, she claimed, not sexual.

porcelain complexion that were to provide her ticket out of Grabtown, North Carolina.

Ava's father was a drinker, her mother a God-fearing Baptist. Life in the small, tobacco-farming town was hard and governed by grinding poverty. After a fire left them homeless, Ava was brought up in a series of boarding houses where her mother cooked to make ends meet. Ava's sense of independence came with her from Grabtown. It was her mother who held the family together, financially and otherwise, while her sister Bappie was also a woman to be reckoned with, divorcing her philandering husband and heading for New York City to get herself a job. Ava never depended on a man in childhood, and although she was often drawn to strong men as an adult she never allowed herself to become dependent on them.

As was the norm in the heyday of Hollywood, Gardner's initial success was determined largely by her extraordinary beauty. She had no experience and her thick southern drawl made her virtually unintelligible, but that could be fixed — the main thing was, she looked the part. "She can't act, she can't talk, but she's a terrific piece of merchandise," said an MGM producer and talent scout after her first screen test.

In true Hollywood fashion Gardner was "spotted" on her first visit to New York. She was eighteen and had gone to visit her sister Bappie, now married to photographer Larry Tarr. Taken with Ava's beauty, Tarr photographed her and placed a picture in his studio window. When an MGM runner expressed interest in the pictures, Tarr decided to send out a batch of portraits to one of the studio's talent scouts. Such was the impact of the pictures that Ava was summmoned to MGM and screen tested the very next day. A silent print was immediately dispatched to Louis B. Mayer, who was so captivated by what he saw that he had her delivered to Hollywood for a second test. In 1941 Metro signed Ava to a seven-year contract and began the process of moulding her into a star. Elocution lessons with leading voice coach Lillian Burns were top of the list.

By the time Ava met Sinatra she had been through the studio starlet system and two whirlwind marriages, first to actor and former child star Mickey Rooney (1942–43), next to bandleader Artie Shaw (1945–46) with a relationship with millionaire aviator and film-maker Howard Hughes spanning both and going on to last twenty years. She had appeared briefly in a string of films, but had yet to make the big time. For better or worse this was to happen during her time with Sinatra.

When she ran into Sinatra again in 1949, Gardner was older and wiser, and his career was in shreds. "A lot of silly stories have been written about what happened to us in Palm Springs, but the truth is more and less exciting," wrote Gardner of the momentous meeting. "We drank, we laughed, we talked and we fell in love . . . We did not kiss or make dates, but we knew, and I think it must have frightened both of us."

She was warned off Sinatra by friend Lana Turner, one of Artie's many wives, who had also had a relationship with Sinatra. Nancy would always come first, warned Turner, and would always be the one he went running back to. Somehow Gardner knew it was different this time. "We became lovers forever — eternally," she said. "Big words, I know. But I truly felt that no matter what happened, we would always be in love."

Although Sinatra had been temporarily separated from Nancy when he met Ava, he continued with his extremely tenuous marriage. After Christina's arrival the whole family had moved to a luxurious new home in Beverly Hills. George Evans, the man who fought hardest to save the marriage, was predicting a happy reunion. A year later the pretence was over.

It was inevitable that an affair between two high-profile celebrities should attract massive media attention. Sinatra had always been careless about his infidelity, but this time he positively flaunted his love for Gardner. For her part, Gardner was only interested in the affair if marriage was on the cards and was keen that Nancy get the message. Against Evans' wishes Sinatra insisted Gardner accompany him on major public engagements, including a fateful show at the Shamrock Hotel in Texas. While dining with the mayor after the show they were snapped by a local photographer and the story broke.

Nancy steadfastly refused to give Sinatra a divorce, doubtless thinking she had heard it all before. Even when he walked out on her she told the press, "I'm not calling it any kind of marital breakup. He will come home." Just weeks later, on Valentine's Day 1950, she found herself issuing a very different press statement, the one she had long dreaded and resisted. "Unfortunately, my married life with Frank has become most unhappy and almost unbearable. We have therefore separated. I have requested my attorney to attempt to work out a property settlement, but I do not contemplate divorce proceedings in the foreseeable future."

Gardner was immediately branded a homewrecker, the Legion of Decency threatened to ban her films and Catholic priests wrote her damning letters. This time there was no George Evans to smooth things out with the press. On 26 January 1950, as Sinatra headed for Houston to begin his two-week stint at the Shamrock, he had received the news that Evans had died, aged forty-eight, of a massive heart attack. Evans had been much more than a press agent to Sinatra. It was a tremendous emotional blow which came in the same week as the resignation of Manie Sachs.

Ava was said to have been drawn to a type: thin, volatile men of Latin extraction. They finally married in 1951.

The relationship between Sinatra and Ava "Hurricane" Gardner was made up of intoxicating highs and bitter lows with little chance to recuperate between dramas. She could not have been less like Nancy. When Frank threw his weight around, she took the first flight out of town. When he forbade her to do something or see somebody he might as well have issued a challenge. The pressure was all the greater because nothing they did was private. As a couple they had almost too much in common. They were both night animals who loved to drink heavily, eat and party into the small hours. She was possibly the first and last woman he met who could match him shot for shot. When things were good they were very, very good. But when things got difficult no emotional holds were barred and their behaviour was childish and hurtful. Despite their success, both were insecure about their lack of education. At the time of their meeting Sinatra was certainly the more vulnerable of the two. He was painfully jealous of the men in Ava's life, and there had been more than a few, often men's men like himself — the most threatening kind to a fallen idol. "Primitive, passionate, bitter, acrimonious, elemental, red-fanged romantic jealousy was our poison," said Ava. "Accusations and counter-accusations were what our quarrels were about." At the same time Ava made it clear that Sinatra's vulnerability was an important part of his appeal.

Together at the premiere of 'Showboat'. Gardner was the star of the moment and Sinatra was on the skids.

If you were in movies, you didn't cross the public. Evans had understood this, Sinatra did not. The "morals" clause in Gardner's MGM contract gives a clear indication of the strength of public opinion on infidelity and divorce in the late Forties: "She will not do or commit any act or thing that will degrade her in society, or bring her into public hatred, contempt, scorn, or ridicule, that will tend to shock, insult, or offend the community or ridicule public morals or decency, or prejudice the producer (MGM) or the motion picture industry in general." As a star in the ascendent, Gardner scraped through. Sinatra, moving in the opposite direction, was not so lucky. In May 1950 MGM dropped him.

With the decline in his film career he turned to television, but Sinatra was never quite cuddly enough for armchair viewing. Where Perry Como, Andy Williams and others consolidated their success on the small screen, it was a medium Sinatra never conquered. He did win a five-year contract with CBS after a guest appearance on the *Bob Hope Show* in 1950 but success was short-lived. When the camera zoomed in on Sinatra it was as if the inner man — tense, angry, bitter, arrogant — was exposed. Ironically it was his guest, Perry Como, who embodied the ideal characteristics and stole the show. Those who worked with Sinatra blamed his lack of respect for the medium and for his co-workers. "He was impossible to work with — absolutely impossible," said one producer, pointing to Sinatra's

preoccupation with Ava, his refusal to rehearse, habitual lateness, misplaced arrogance and tendency to turn on those around him. It wasn't long before the sponsors pulled out and Sinatra's contract with CBS was cancelled.

But nothing hurt Sinatra as much as his falling out with Columbia Records. Losing his movie contract was one thing, but failing in his career as a musician was certainly something he had never contemplated. Above and beyond his problems with Miller, Sinatra's voice had been affected by his turbulent personal life. The elegantly sustained phrasing for which he was famous suffered under the strain and his vocal range narrowed. At the same time, recordings from this difficult period reveal new emotional depths which more than compensate for any technical failings. Music journalist George T. Simon described "I'm a Fool to Want You", recorded early in 1951, as "the most emotional side of Frank I've ever heard". Sinatra co-wrote the song with friend and music publisher Ben Barton at a time when Ava was refusing to see him. Barton was in the studio on the day. "It was terribly emotional, Frank was really worked up. He did the song in one take; then he just turned around and walked out of the studio, and that was it."

Despite showing a return to form with some fine songs in his last years at Columbia — "You Do Something to Me", "My Blue Heaven" and the buoyant "Birth of the Blues" — the relationship ended on a sour note. The singer left owing over $10,000 in unearned advances and without the prospect of a new contract elsewhere. He knew how to bear a grudge and never stopped blaming Mitch Miller for his problems at Columbia. It was Miller, he said, who had consistently provided him with unsuitable material, citing novelty single "Mama Will Bark" (a duet accompanied by dog impressions), as a convincing example. Many years after leaving Columbia Sinatra bumped into Miller at the Sands Hotel, Las Vegas. A mutual friend ushered Miller over to Sinatra's table, saying it was time for the two to make amends, but as Miller offered his hand, Sinatra's response was a curt "Fuck you, keep walking."

With the crumbling of the studio system and the strength of the American dollar, more and more films were being made overseas. Ava's new film, *Pandora and the Flying Dutchman*, was to be shot in Spain, but before leaving she followed Sinatra to New York. Sinatra had been surviving on appearances in small-time venues and allegedly calling in favours from underworld friends. Unbelievably, he was in financial trouble. He had never saved and the little he still had coming in was withheld pending the maintenance settlement with Nancy. That March, 1950, he began a run at the Copa, his first big nightclub appearance for some time. His nerves were in tatters and his voice in danger of disappearing altogether. Despite continuing

Frank and Ava in Spain with friends, including Jimmy Van Heusen.

Fans were more forgiving in London, where Ava was filming, and Sinatra stopped over to play the Palladium.

press attacks, Ava accompanied him to every show. It was a tense time which exploded into melodrama when Ava went to a party at Artie Shaw's apartment. An enraged Sinatra phoned the party, demanded to speak to Ava and proceeded to threaten suicide, firing a series of pistol shots into his hotel mattress for dramatic effect. The point had been made and the couple made up. "Frank and I never mentioned the incident again," said Gardner. "Post mortems were not our style."

A few days later Gardner left for Spain, stopping en route in England to take care of post-production details. It was her first trip to Europe. She felt so comfortable in London that she was to spend the second half of her life there, but it was in Spain that she discovered a spiritual home.

'Meet Danny Wilson', in which Sinatra starred opposite Shelley Winters. The two volatile personalities clashed: she reportedly called him a "stupid Hoboken bastard", and he called her "a bow legged bitch".

Although Gardner called Mario Cabre, her co-star in *Pandora*, "a Spanish pain in the ass, better at self-promotion than either bullfighting or love", this didn't stop her falling into bed with him. "A single mistake," she said, "which turned into a blunder of major proportions." Unfortunately, it was a mistake Cabre was keen to recount to the world's press. There were rumours that the affair was Ava's revenge for Sinatra's failure to push Nancy into a divorce. Whatever her motivation, Sinatra had been openly betrayed. The impact was swift and devastating. In the midst of the run at the

Copa, he cancelled five performances and, on returning for the sixth, he lost his voice. The Copa announced that he had suffered a throat haemorrhage and had been ordered to take two weeks' rest. He flew straight to Spain, pursued by panting press men.

The couple reconciled and returned to the States, where negotiations with Nancy continued. Desperate to be free, Sinatra allowed Nancy's lawyers to take him to the cleaners, but she still denied him the divorce he needed to hold on to Ava.

Ava's career continued to move upwards as she started work on *Showboat*. Sinatra had to content himself with TV work described disparagingly in the *New York Times* as "a drab mixture of radio, routine vaudeville and pallid pantomime". Meanwhile, Sinatra and Gardner were a constant target for the gossip columnists. "Nothing we did was too inconsequential for the ever-present swarm of reporters and photographers to feed on like bees at a honey pot," said Gardner of the situation. "It's very easy to say we should have accepted this as the price of fame, but that turns out to be a hell of a tall order to live up to when you practically can't go to the bathroom without finding yourself on page one."

At this stage Ava issued her ultimatum: get a divorce or I won't see you. Little wonder that Sinatra's involvement in *Meet Danny Wilson* was noticeably half-hearted. It was the last film he made on

In 'Meet Danny Wilson' Sinatra plays a nightclub singer with Mob connections.

To score the film, DJs across the country were asked to poll listeners for the songs Wilson and Sinatra should sing.

his way down and his performance was belittled on the grounds that he was yet again playing himself. The parallels are hard to ignore. He plays a nightclub singer indebted for his success to a crooked club owner. It's not a bad film and under other circumstances Sinatra's performance might have been received differently. As it was, the public and the studios had already lost faith. Co-star Shelley Winters remembers the difficulties on set — tearful phone calls from Nancy, Sinatra's children visiting him on set along with priests from the Catholic Family Counselling Service — and described him as "so disturbed that he couldn't hear anything anyone said to him". She also remembers his unacceptable rudeness and temper tantrums.

In May 1951 Nancy finally agreed in theory to a divorce saying it was "the only way for my happiness as well as Frank's". It is possible she detected a change in public opinion and a growing sympathy for the frustrated lovers. If so, it was to be short-lived. Two months later Sinatra hit the headlines following what was reported as a violent attack on a journalist. Sinatra and Gardner had decided to leave town for a holiday in Acapulco. With rumours that they were actually planning to marry in Mexico they were dogged by press from Los Angeles via El Paso to Mexico City and back. By the time they returned to Los Angeles, having begged for privacy at every stop, Sinatra was spoiling for a fight. In the mêlée at the airport, he tried a quick escape and was subsequently accused of driving at high speed into a group of photographers, sideswiping one and threatening to kill him. The photographer demanded and received a letter of apology, although Gardner later claimed the man had deliberately thrown himself on to the bonnet.

Only days later Sinatra made the headlines again. This time he was said to have attempted suicide after a fight with Ava during a long weekend at Lake Tahoe. Reports claimed he had overdosed on sleeping pills but was found by his valet. Sinatra said it was an allergic reaction to mild medication combined with alcohol and dismissed it as a silly mistake.

In October '51 the divorce finally came through. Within twenty-four hours Sinatra and Gardner had applied for a marriage licence allowing them to marry a few days later. Despite efforts to mislead the press, they were tracked down and Sinatra had a final row before leaving for his honeymoon in Cuba. During a stop-over in Miami they were photographed, strolling arm in arm on a deserted beach, backs to the camera. They look happy but at the same time isolated by their circumstances, turning their backs on the outside world and inwards towards each other.

Although Sinatra and Gardner had achieved their immediate goal, circumstances were not on their side. *Showboat* made Ava a star. Frank had hit rock bottom and was financially dependent on her.

Axel Stordahl was best man when the couple finally tied the knot. Ava was the first bride Dolly really took to. Attempts to outsmart the press failed.

Ava with idol Clark Gable on the set of 'Mogambo', famously filmed on location in the African jungle.

It was Ava who was accorded the ultimate Hollywood honour and asked to leave her hand prints in the concrete outside Graumans' Chinese Theatre. Frank would have to wait another thirteen years. For a man so concerned with machismo, this cannot have been easy to bear.

Married as unmarried, their relationship followed the familiar pattern. "The problems were never in the bedroom," said Ava later with characteristic frankness. "We were always great in bed. The trouble usually started on the way to the bidet." 1952 was also election year and as Frank and Ava pledged their support for Democratic nominee Adlai Stevenson, Sinatra's old press enemies renewed their attacks.

Next stop for Ava was Africa and the filming of *Mogambo*, literally a dream come true. Gardner had sneaked into the theatre balcony as a child in Smithfield, Virginia, to swoon over her hero Clark Gable in *Red Dust*. Now, twenty years later, she was starring opposite him in a remake of that same film. Sinatra, with no other commitments, went along with her, returning off and on for performances in the States. Although Ava was loyal and supportive in practical terms, she was not the kind of person to provide the ego-stroking he needed. Besides, she had her hands full building her own career.

Sinatra was on his own. His agents, MCA, had long ago lost interest in promoting him and eventually dropped him, claiming he owed them $40,000 in back commissions. Without an agency he set about generating his own publicity, arranging a two-week run at the Paramount to coincide with the opening of *Meet Danny Wilson*. Where adoring crowds had once jammed the aisles, most seats now remained empty. "Gone on Frankie in '42. Gone in '52" ran the headlines. Weeks later he pulled in only 150 people to the 1,200-seater Chez Paree in Chicago. And despite his desperate efforts, *Meet Danny Wilson* made little impact. He certainly didn't look like a man who would win an Oscar three years later.

The honeymoon couple in Miami, turning their backs on press and public.

CHAPTER FIVE

FROM ETERNITY TO THE CAPITOL YEARS, 1953

Before leaving for Africa Sinatra played his last card. He had seen a part he wanted, a part he felt he was born to play. The part was Private Angelo Maggio. The film was *From Here to Eternity*.

The film, based on a James Jones novel, is set in Hawaii during World War II and tells the story of Robert E. Lee Prewitt (Montgomery Clift), a hard-headed loner at odds with army life. His only friend and ally is the tough little private, Angelo Maggio, who later dies in his arms after a vicious beating from a sadistic sergeant.

Maggio — a rebellious Italian-American with a big heart, raised in the slums of the Depression, cocky, fast talking, constantly fighting the system and determined not to let it break him — was only fifth billing, but Sinatra knew he could make it his own. "I knew Maggio," he said with genuine conviction. "I went to high school with him in Hoboken. I was beaten up with him. I might have been Maggio."

His instincts told him to go all out for the role even though Broadway actor Eli Wallach had already been pencilled in for it and was known to be the first choice of director Fred Zinnemann. Sinatra had to hustle as he had in the early days. He used every contact he had so that the head of Columbia, Harry Cohn, was inundated with pleas on Sinatra's behalf. When these were dismissed, Ava took his case to Cohn's wife Joan. She begged Joan to persuade her husband at least to grant Sinatra a screen test, saying she thought he might kill himself if he did not get the part. This was a brave and unorthodox move on Ava's part. Cohn was a particularly unapproachable man of whom it was said "you had to stand in line to hate him." The intervention could have blown up in Ava's face, but fortunately Joan Cohn sympathized and promised to put a word in for Sinatra. Before leaving for Nairobi, Sinatra made a final attempt to persuade Cohn, only to be told, "Look, Frank. Maggio is an actor's part. You're a singer, not an actor.' Even Sinatra's offer to play the part for $1,000 a week, a fraction of the normal fee, was not yet enough to sway Cohn.

While Burt Lancaster, Montgomery Clift, Deborah Kerr and Donna Reed got the go-ahead, Sinatra was left to sweat in Africa.

Nairobi, 1952. Ava was working, Frank was along for the ride.

Sinatra needed a miracle, and found it in 'From Here to Eternity'.

Maggio was the last part to be cast. At last, for whatever reasons, Cohn decided to give him a screen test. Returning immediately, Sinatra did two scenes without a script and his performance made an immediate and dramatic impact on Zinnemann. "You'd better come down here," he told producer Buddy Adler on the phone. "You'll see something unbelievable." With both Zinnemann and Adler convinced, it remained only for Cohn to give his consent, which he did shortly afterwards. There are various explanations for Cohn's change of heart; some maintain that Eli Wallach turned the part down in favour of a prestigious theatre role or that Harry Cohn left the final decision to his wife, who felt the small, wiry Sinatra was physically right for the part; others say simply that Cohn was loath to pay $20,000 to Wallach when Sinatra was happy to do it for $8,000. There was one rumour everyone was keen to scotch, however — the story later popularized by the film adaptation of Mario Puzo's novel *The Godfather*. In the film, Johnny Fontane, a famous Italian singer, asks his friend, a Mafia don, to help him get a role for which he has been turned down. He needs to relaunch his career and knows he is made for the part. The don duly makes the request on Fontane's behalf, but fails to persuade the powerful studio head. A few days later the studio boss awakes to find the decapitated head of his most highly prized racehorse alongside him in bed. He gives Fontane the part. Although *The Godfather* is a work of fiction, Fontane was generally assumed to be a thinly disguised portait of Sinatra. This added to his reputation as a friend of the Mob, although he successfully sued the BBC for suggesting that he won the part with their help and all those associated with *From Here To Eternity* dismissed the story as preposterous.

Sinatra with co-stars Donna Reed and Montgomery Clift. The rushes were so promising that Harry Cohn pushed the film out ahead of time.

Private Maggio, a role in a million and tailor made for Sinatra.

It was the relationship
between Sinatra and
Clift, on and off screen,
that stole the show. "I
learned more from him
acting," says Sinatra,
"than I ever
knew before".

The triumphant Sinatra applied himself as never before to the process of film-making. There was none of his customary impatience and arrogance. Both Adler and Zinnemann gained new respect for Sinatra. "He played Maggio so spontaneously we almost never had to reshoot a scene," said Zinnemann, while Adler unwittingly picked up on Sinatra's musicality, saying "He has the most amazing sense of timing and occasionally he'll drop in a word or two that makes the line actually bounce."

Thanks to the chemistry between Clift and Sinatra, an otherwise perfect cast and Zinnemann's lean, intelligent direction, the film went on to become the most successful of 1953. It won the hearts of the critics, the New York Film Critics giving it Best Film, Best Actor (Lancaster) and Best Director; the public, who made it Columbia's biggest ever earner and kept cinemas open around the clock; and the industry, who nominated all five lead players and awarded it eight Oscars — Best Film, Direction, Screenplay, Photography, Editing, Sound, Supporting Actress (Donna Reed) and Supporting Actor (Frank Sinatra). The film's theme, expressed most succinctly by Prewitt — "If a man don't go his own way, he's nuthin'" — hit an American chord. *Time* felt it told a truth "about life, about the inviolability of the human spirit".

It is ironic that Sinatra's renaissance came about through film, a medium for which he had previously shown a consistent lack of respect. Known as one-take Sinatra, he had no interest in the mechanics of film and no patience with the process, often treating his fellow actors and technicians with contempt. His approach to film work was in complete contrast with his approach to recording, where he took endless care to achieve perfection, often re-recording whole songs to improve on a single vowel sound or emphasis. His 1954 recording of "Day In, Day Out", for instance, was the result of thirty-one takes. For the first time, with *Eternity,* he brought to the screen the depth and sensitivity that characterized his singing.

The film picked up eight Oscars.

The film not only led to critical recognition as an actor, it helped Sinatra regain confidence, energy and a sense of creative motivation. "It was like watching a man grow day by day," said a member of the production crew." . . . he kind of filled out and his head went back and he started looking you straight in the eye again. And when he walked off at the end of the picture, he walked out like he was king once more."

The next seven years were to be the most exciting and creative of Sinatra's career. But first there was a waiting period to be endured between the making and the release of *Eternity.* He signed with Capitol Records while the film was still in production. It was only a one-year contract, there was no advance and Sinatra had to pay all his own expenses, including orchestra and arranger. Axel Stordahl helped pave the way and arranged Sinatra's first two singles in April 1953, "I'm Walking Behind You" and the fabulous "Lean Baby". But when the time came to step aside shortly afterwards, Stordahl did so graciously. It was then, under the guidance of Capitol producer Voyle Gilmore, that Sinatra teamed up with Nelson Riddle, the man with the sound to launch Sinatra into the Fifties. Although Frank sometimes worked with Billy May and Gordon Jenkins, the Riddle-Sinatra partnership defined the period of his career known as the Capitol Years.

By the time Sinatra completed his second batch of recordings for Capitol, including "South of the Border", "Don't Worry About Me" and "My One and Only Love", the new swinging Sinatra had replaced the crooner of the Forties. In place of Stordahl's lush, dreamy strings came a hipper, sharper, more rhythmic sound. "It was the particular confluence of brass, reeds and strings which gave the sound and style their own unique flavour," said *Times* music critic and biographer Derek Jewell, "each reacting to the other, so it seemed, the blare never too extreme, the softness never too cloying, and the whole sustained by a bounding beat in the faster numbers, and a pulse which is unescapable even in the slower ones."

On the home front things were as rocky as ever. Sinatra and Gardner had been spending a lot of time apart due to separate career commitments. Filming *Mogambo* on location in the jungle had been difficult enough for Ava. She had also undergone two abortions in quick succession, feeling that her lifestyle and relationship at the time were not right for children. Finally, an attempted second honeymoon in Europe had been an unmitigated disaster, with Sinatra playing to angry audiences in half-empty venues and tangling with the press.

Sinatra's press statements on his marriage were confused. "I can't make a statement because I don't know what she's planning," he said, giving away the power balance in the relationship. "It's a crying shame, because everything was going so well with us. Something may work out but I don't know." Ava's were increasingly pessimistic. "When he was down and out he was sweet. Now that he's got successful again, he's become his old arrogant self. We were happy when he was on the skids."

On 29 October 1953, just weeks after the première of *Mogambo,* MGM broke the news: "Ava Gardner and Frank Sinatra stated today that having reluctantly exhausted every effort to reconcile their differences, they could find no mutual basis on which to continue their marriage. Both expressed deep regret and great respect for each other. Their separation is final and Miss Gardner will seek a divorce."

Sinatra fell to pieces. Ava's response to trouble was to make a run for it, heading for Rome to film *The Barefoot Contessa.* They communicated via the press. Things reached a head in November when Sinatra was hospitalized. According to the official version he was suffering from complete physical exhaustion and severe weight loss, but others speculated about another suicide attempt. Musically, he laid himself bare as never before. Songs like "Don't Worry 'Bout Me" and "There Will Never Be Another You" reflected his despair, giving him another dimension as a man and a musician. Nelson Riddle said later that losing the love of his life was what really taught Sinatra to sing a torch song.

Although Sinatra refused to accept that the breakdown of the marriage was irreparable, Gardner's brief but well-publicized affair with Spanish idol and world-famous bullfighter Luis Miguel Dominguin effectively sealed the breach. The divorce didn't become final until 1957 and they continued to see each other sporadically for many years. "Every once in a while Frank would call me in Madrid, London, Rome, New York, wherever I happened to be, and say, 'Ava, let's try again.' And I'd say, 'Okay' and drop everything, sometimes even a part in a picture. And it would be heaven, but it wouldn't last more than twenty-four hours. And I'd go running off again, literally running. We could never really understand why it hadn't and couldn't work out."

As the relationship with
Ava gradually broke
down, Sinatra retreated
to the studio.

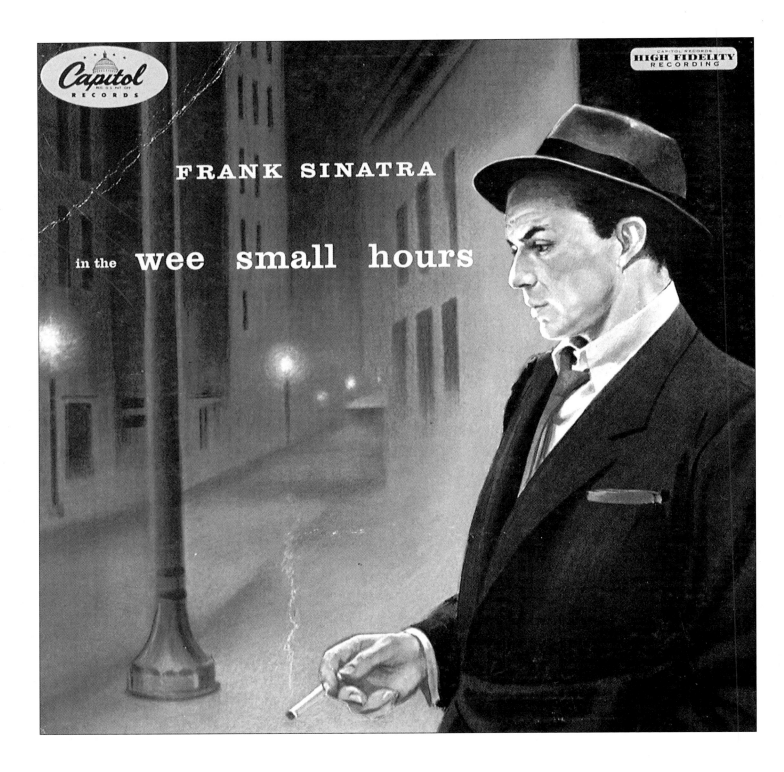

CHAPTER SIX

BACK TO BUSINESS, 1954

Sinatra's music moved from heartbreaking torchsongs to buoyant bachelor anthems.

"The greatest change in my life began the night they gave me the Oscar," said Sinatra of his moment of glory. He was a popular choice for Best Supporting Actor. All the world loves an underdog and as one cynical Hollywood columnist pointed out, "He proved you could flop and make a comeback", something his peers found pleasantly reassuring. As Sinatra gratefully acknowledged the appropriate people, it's possible he felt more like expressing other emotions, emotions of bitterness and vindication. Here he was with the industry at his feet when only a few years ago the same people wouldn't give him the time of day. The second time around he was to be more careful, less willing to leave himself vulnerable. It was from this moment on that he started to do things his way.

With newfound credibility as a serious actor and an Academy Award under his belt, it would have been easy for Sinatra to concentrate on his film career. But this was an area where even the most talented individual could have little control. While he kept it afloat and made a wise choice for his next film, *Suddenly,* he immersed himself in music. As well as new emotional depth, Sinatra had a new authority, the punchy, almost cocky air of a man who has suffered and survived.

On a good day the Capitol studios in the mid Fifties offered front-row seats to the most intimate of Sinatra performances. His inner circle were invited and at centre stage stood the Sinatra reproduced on countless album covers: snap-brim hat pushed back on the head, tie loosened and smoke spiralling from the obligatory cigarette. He preferred to record in the evening after eight and usually called it a day around midnight. On average they would record three or four numbers a session, but the magical single takes are the stuff of musical legend. "One For My Baby" was just such a moment. Over sixty people, including friends and technicians, were in the studio when producer Dave Cavanaugh blacked out the room, leaving only a spotlight on Sinatra. The studio was transformed into a club and the track recorded in one straight take. The song remains a staple of

After 'Eternity', Sinatra moved into the most creative musical period of his career, recording with Billy May and Nelson Riddle, described by Sinatra as "the greatest arranger in the world".

Sinatra's performances and seems to improve with age. It's a perfect showcase for Sinatra the actor and communicator; a chance to tell a classic story of lost love, autobiographical but universal, epitomizing an ordinary Joe like no other singer before or since.

As Sinatra made his comeback, the eight-track long-playing album was just coming into its own. Ever the musical innovator, Sinatra realized its potential and pioneered the concept album. Having decided on a theme, often drawn from experience, that he wanted to explore in depth, he would whittle down a short list of sixty or so songs to the definitive group. From there the pace and running order would be decided on, something Sinatra seemed to do with intuitive ease. Albums like *In the Wee Small Hours* and *Come Fly With Me* are perfect examples: the first tells of his aching personal disappointment and grief at losing Ava, the second asks listeners to share in his rebirth, renewed confidence and zest for life.

Each of his arrangers added a different flavour to the mix presided over by Sinatra, but his most consistent partner was Riddle. The partnership was special not only because they shared a common approach to music, but because their personalities complemented one another so well. Riddle describes himself as calm and patient, characteristics vital to a successful working relationship with Sinatra and which helped theirs last off and on for twenty-five years. "I don't argue," Riddle has said. "I hold my temper too long, but that's why I could work with Frank, I guess." Sinatra could be unpredictable and aggressive, sometimes shoving Riddle aside to take over conducting when he was unhappy with the way things were going. But, despite Sinatra's demanding nature, Riddle recognized him as a perfectionist who drove others only as hard as he drove himself and tended to bring out the best in fellow musicians.

"He's stimulating to work with," said Riddle. "You have to be right on the mettle all the time. The man himself somehow draws everything out of you. He has the same effect on the boys in the band — they know he means business, so they pull everything out. Frank and I both have, I think, the same musical aim. We know what we're each doing with a song, what we want the song to say . . . In working out arrangements for Frank, I suppose we stuck to two main rules. First — find the peak of the song and build the whole arrangement to that peak, pacing it as he paces himself vocally. Second — when he's moving, get the hell out of the way; when he's doing nothing, move in fast and establish something. After all what arranger in his right mind would try to fight *against* Sinatra's voice?"

Despite his cool exterior, Riddle shared Sinatra's passion for music as well as his natural understanding of how to connect with an audience. "Our best albums together were *Songs for Swingin' Lovers, A Swingin' Affair* and *Only the Lonely*," said Riddle. "Most of our best

Riddle's personal favourites, albums no record collection should be without.

Sinatra's fifties recording sessions were legendary.

numbers were in what I call the tempo of the heartbeat. That's the tempo that strikes people easiest because, without their knowing it, they are moving to that pace all their working hours. Music to me is sex," he went on. "It's all tied up somehow, and the rhythm of sex is the heartbeat. I always have some woman in mind for each song I arrange."

While the album offered the perfect format for Sinatra's long-term success, the singles market was vital to the relaunching of his music career. The same month as the Oscars ceremony, "Young at Heart" rocketed to the top of the charts and stayed there for the next twenty weeks. After that the honours rolled in: he took *Metronome's* singer of the year; *Billboard's* critics poll for best single ("Young at Heart"), best album (*Swing Easy*) and best singer; and, for the first time in seven years, he was voted Down Beat's best male vocalist. He also had limited success with *Suddenly,* in which he plays an out-and-out villain, a psychopathic assassin, weak but empowered by a gun, lying in wait for the President. Again Sinatra had opted for a straight role in an interesting if not particularly commercial movie.

All in all 1954 was a very good year for Sinatra. So good that he took a full page ad in *Billboard* at the end of the year listing his many achievements, awards and ongoing film projects. It was signed "Busy, busy, busy — Frank".

That same year Sinatra also began a lifetime link with casinos that was to make him a millionaire, buying a two per cent stake in the Sands Hotel, Las Vegas. During the hearing necessary to grant him a Nevada state gambling licence he was asked, not for the last time, about his ties with organized crime, but managed to persuade the board that his intentions were entirely legitimate. After a year of scrutiny and indecision he was granted the all-important licence. Whether or not Sinatra himself was involved with gangsters, they were certainly involved with the casino business (Bugsy Seigel already owned the Flamingo, one of the first casinos to open in Las Vegas) and the mutual benefits of friendship were high. Gangsters were in a position to offer favours — a stake in the business or a regular spot in a high-profile venue — and stars like Sinatra were in a position to pull in the big spenders and other top performers. Certainly in the case of the Sands, Sinatra drew enormous crowds over the years, making huge sums of money for those at the top. In return he was treated like a king on the loose in his private kingdom. Staff remained appropriately subservient regardless of his often atrocious behaviour, friends were given five-star treatment and Sinatra was given free reign to indulge his passion for gambling.

Suddenly had shown that *Eternity* was no flash in the pan and Sinatra now felt comfortable about returning to a musical. In *Young at Heart*, he teamed up with Doris Day in a standard boy-gets-girl, boy-

'Suddenly', not big box office, but a respectable follow-up to his Oscar-winning performance.

'Not as a Stranger' met with a thumbs down from the critics but he redeemed himself with a virtuoso perfomance in 'The Man with the Golden Arm'.

loses-girl, boy-gets-girl tearjerker in which Sinatra's songs — "Young at Heart", "Someone to Watch Over Me", "Just One of Those Things" and "One for My Baby" — lift the film above average. He followed with *Not as a Stranger*, a Stanley Kramer film starring Robert Mitchum and Olivia de Havilland, in which Sinatra plays a wise-cracking, cynical young doctor. The film was written off as an up-market soap opera, but again Sinatra in his supporting role was singled out for praise.

With renewed confidence and success came fresh outbursts and physical confrontations. He was involved in a nightclub scuffle in which he punched press agent Jim Byron. Byron claimed he had been attacked, Sinatra pleaded self-defence. He was also involved in a series of lawsuits: one against an English newspaper group for libel and another against producer Sam Spiegel, who he claimed had promised him the role of Terry Molloy in *On the Waterfront,* the part that won Marlon Brando the Oscar that year.

Sinatra was still deeply unsettled by the end of his relationship with Ava. Rumours had him surrounding himself with photographs of her and drinking himself to sleep. One story told of a distraught Sinatra tearing up his favourite picture of Ava one night. Immediately regretting it, he desperately gathered up the pieces to find one was missing — her nose —which only reappeared near the doorway when a mystified delivery boy arrived with a crate of booze and found himself being rewarded with Sinatra's gold wristwatch.

In 1955 the restless Sinatra continued at a frenetic pace, making *The Tender Trap, Guys and Dolls* and *The Man with the Golden Arm*. Already in the planning stage were *Johnny Concho, High Society, The Pride and the Passion, The Joker is Wild* and *Pal Joey*. "All these wonderful roles came together," he said, "but I don't call it a comeback. I wasn't away anywhere."

The Tender Trap did well at the box office with Sinatra perfectly cast as the smooth-talking womanizer, the prototype for his swinging bachelor persona. It also spawned another hit title song by Jimmy Van Heusen and Sammy Cahn. But at this stage Sinatra needed a big commercial and critical hit to keep him at the top. *Guys and Dolls* was the one to do it, although it got off to a bad start when Sinatra once again lost the lead to Brando, the man he variously called "Mumbles" and "the most over-rated actor in the world". Brando was cast against type in the romantic singing role more obviously suited to Sinatra, while Sinatra was left to play Nathan Detroit, proprietor of "the oldest established permanent floating crap game in New York". Against the odds, Sinatra made sure the casting worked in his favour, his detailed characterization giving an extra dimension to an otherwise highly stylized production.

'Young at Heart'. The title song went to number one.

Hands-on direction from Otto Preminger on the set of 'The Man with the Golden Arm'.

The resulting romantic comedy belies the off-screen tension between Method actor Brando and "one take" Sinatra. Its success relied heavily on director Joe Mankiewicz's skilful manipulation of the two men, using the competitive friction between them to his advantage. While critical opinion may have been mixed, it was a popular success and went on to become a classic of the genre.

Finally for 1955, in a very different vein, came Frankie Machine in *The Man with the Golden Arm*, a very unAmerican film dealing realistically with the desperation of heroin addiction. The role of a junkie at his lowest ebb is one few leading men of the day would have risked taking. Rumour has it that Brando was the other name being mooted for the part, which itself may have made it more appealing to Sinatra. At the same time it fitted in with his image as a kid from the streets who wanted to help others on to the right path. "There were a couple of older guys on the block who acted kinda funny," Sinatra remembered. "Later I found out they were on junk. In poor, tough neighbourhoods like that, one pedlar can ruin a lot of kids' lives."

It was certainly as close as mainstream American cinema had come to social realism with an explicit and ugly portrayal of drug use set against the grimy backdrop of a poor, urban subculture many Americans preferred not to acknowledge. The film chronicles Frankie's desperate struggle to overcome his drug habit and build a new life despite having to return to the same haunts, the same crowd and the same temptations on his release from prison. Inside, he has discovered a talent for drums and has a one-off chance to try out with a band. But everything seems to conspire against him and his gradual collapse is emotionally draining to watch. His addiction is an itch that has to be scratched, a feeling of unbearable frustration that Sinatra conveys with grim intensity as he finally succumbs to his old dealer and follows him like a dog towards his fix.

Director Otto Preminger's intention was to make a fast-moving, commercial movie while maintaining the depressing reality of drug abuse, a tricky combination. Sinatra's performance was much praised, but even with the addition of a happy ending the film was far from standard box-office material (in the novel on which it is based Frankie loses the fight against drugs and commits suicide; in the film he gets the girl and a new start). In England opinion was dramatically, if predictably, divided. "A magnificent film," said the *Spectator*. "Sinatra has never in his life given a better performance . . . Brilliantly directed, this is a shattering, notable film." The *Express* did not agree, describing it hysterically as, "another of those violent, tawdry, scum-ridden films which appeal to the baser instincts by showing human beings rolling around in squalor and filth".

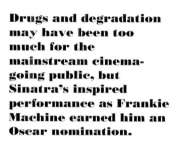

Drugs and degradation may have been too much for the mainstream cinema-going public, but Sinatra's inspired performance as Frankie Machine earned him an Oscar nomination.

Face to face – one-take Sinatra and method actor Marlon Brando. Brando got the lead singing role but Sinatra had his revenge – years later he would introduce "Luck be a Lady" by saying "I made a movie once and who did they get to sing this song? A bum who couldn't sing".

Sinatra earned himself a nomination for best actor and he and Preminger parted on very good terms. They had worked well together — so well that when Paramount offered Preminger the chance to direct *The Godfather*, Sinatra was his first and only choice for Don Corleone. When Sinatra passed, it went to Francis Ford Coppola and Brando.

In 1955 Sinatra held on to his top spot in the *Metronome*, *Down Beat* and *Billboard* polls as number one male vocalist. With the release of the bittersweet "In the Wee Small Hours", a critical and popular success, he also found acceptance among jazz critics. "Sinatra has always had a taste and an intuition for jazz nuances, for improvisational ornaments, for swinging beats, far beyond the call of popular singing," said one impressed critic.

By now rock and roll had established that it was here to stay. Bill Haley and the Comets had crashed into the charts in 1954, followed by Chuck Berry and Little Richard; and by 1956 Elvis had taken teenage America by storm with "Heartbreak Hotel". Sinatra made a respectable attempt at rhythm and blues with "Two Hearts, Two Kisses", but for the most part he didn't enjoy the new sound, describing it in 1957 as an "ugly, degenerate, vicious form of expression" which fostered "almost totally negative and destructive

Duetting with daughter Nancy, and preparing for the inaugural gala with songwriter Jimmy Van Heusen.

Recording the songs for 'Young at Heart' with arranger Ray Heindorf.

reactions in young people". For a man in his forties with teenage daughters this view was far from unusual. Again, there was much about Sinatra that the man in the street could relate to. Surprisingly, it was only really in the singles market that the new sound was a threat and even there singles like "Love and Marriage", "Learnin' the Blues" and "Hey, Jealous Lover" still fared well. Sinatra's LPs continued to have a huge impact, seemingly unaffected by the new pretenders. The superbly punchy and confident *Songs for Swingin' Lovers* was an enormous success and made *Metronome's* album of the year for 1956. The younger audience may have found new idols, but older listeners, particularly middle-aged men, identified happily with Sinatra the swinger, closer to their age but still irrefutably cool.

His prolific film output had already earned him the title King of Hollywood; now Sinatra moved to reclaim his position as King ofClubs. Immaculate in tuxedo and trimmings he offered highly personal interpretations of Tin Pan Alley's finest — George Gershwin, Richard Rodgers, Irving Berlin, Cole Porter — and originals from their natural successors — Sammy Cahn, Jimmy Van Heusen and Jule Styne. He was singing the music he loved as well as establishing a career that would be immune to the unpredictable fads and fashions of popular music.

Inevitably, perhaps, for someone churning out so many films, Sinatra made quite a few duds. One of these was the cowboy movie *Johnny Concho,* his fifth film in only thirteen months and the first which he also produced. The same year Sinatra also made *The Pride and the Passion* in which he plays a Spanish peasant leader. It was a big budget adventure spectacle and, although kind to Sinatra, *Time* said snidely of the film, "It evidently takes more than dedication, co-operative multitudes and $4 millon to shoot history in the face."

There were the usual problems on set. Sinatra insisted on commuting from Madrid at huge expense rather than roughing it on location in rural Spain with the rest of the cast and crew. "Frank is a tremendously talented man, intuitive and fast," said Stanley Kramer, echoing the words of many directors before him, "which is good for him but not always for the rest of the actors." It was the worst type of film for Sinatra: a cast of thousands, epic action scenes and all the problems of location shooting. The tension was made worse by Sinatra's proximity to Ava, who still lived in Spain.

Fortunately there was a lighter side to 1956. *High Society* was great fun to make and a box-office smash, and *Around the World in Eighty Days,* in which Sinatra was one of forty celebrities to take a tiny cameo role, was perfect for him, requiring little time or effort. In *High Society*, Bing Crosby, Grace Kelly and Sinatra give some of the best performances of their careers, although Cole Porter's songs — including "Well, Did You Evah?, What a Swell Party This Is", "True Love" and "Who Wants to be a Millionaire?" — are the real stars of the show, with all the wittiest and most romantic lines. In her last screen role, Kelly gives her most relaxed performance, and Sinatra and Crosby, whose contrasting styles earned themselves the on-set nicknames Dexedrine and Nembutal (pep-up and chill-out drugs respectively), work perfectly together as a sophisticated musical comedy team.

As one of over forty guest stars in 'Around the World in Eighty Days', and as a peasant in 'The Pride and the Passion'. Critics made more of his ludicrous hairstyle than his performance.

Somehow in that very busy year Sinatra managed a move to a palatial, custom-built home in Coldwater Canyon, Hollywood. From his house perched high in the hills, the King of Hollywood could look down on his kingdom. It was the clubhouse for his entourage but a fortress from the outside world. On the entrance gate was a daunting sign reading, "If you haven't been invited, you better have a damn good reason for ringing this bell."

While his film career continued to soar with more hits than misses, his personal reputation was not good. The most public of his fights with the industry was his disagreement with his old friend Ed Sullivan over an appearance fee. Sinatra felt he was owed for a spot on Sullivan's show to promote *Guys and Dolls*. Sullivan argued that a plug which benefited the actor should be free and when Sinatra took his complaint to the Screen Actors' Guild, Sullivan published an open letter to Sinatra in *Variety*. Sullivan, who had always supported Sinatra even through the hard times, reminded him of his words back in 1947: "Ed, you can have my last drop of blood." Sinatra responded with his own page in Variety, foolishly giving way to his most juvenile instincts: "Dear Ed, you are sick — Frankie. PS — Sick, sick, sick."

Cole Porter was paid 250,000 dollars to write nine original songs for 'High Society', and he earned every penny of it twice over.

Sinatra's next two films took him back to familiar territory. *The Joker is Wild* is the true story of singer-turned-comedian Joe E. Lewis, whose trademarks were his cynical humour and drunken delivery. Caught in a battle between competing racketeers his vocal chords are slashed when he switches allegiance from one club to another. After sinking into self-pity, becoming an alcoholic and losing his friends, he finally picks himself up and starts the long, hard journey to recovery and success. It was a great story and produced a natural performance from Sinatra as well as two great songs, "Chicago" and "All the Way", which won Cahn and Van Heusen the Academy Award for Best Song of 1957.

In *Pal Joey*, filmed in early 1957, Sinatra again plays a singer, but this time a fast-talking heel who finds himself pursued by two women: wealthy Rita Hayworth and nightclub newcomer Kim Novak. Unfortunately the film is a watered-down version of the original play and Broadway musical (in which Gene Kelly played Joey), with a hard-to-swallow happy ending tacked on. The play was simply too risqué and low on the moral values being promoted by Hollywood at the time. In the film, much of the original spice and grit is lost, as is the original characterization of Joey as a second-rate singer, leaving behind another performance by Sinatra as Sinatra. Although many of the original songs were also dropped, a few fabulous numbers remain, including "The Lady is a Tramp",

sung to Hayworth by Sinatra seated at the piano in the eerie stillness of an empty music hall. Despite unflattering comparisons with the original, the film was one of Columbia's biggest ever musical hits. This was good news for the star, whose own independent production company had a stake in both *Pal Joey* and *The Joker is Wild*. Sinatra the businessman was diversifying and accumulating.

The year that had begun tragically with the death of close friend Humphrey Bogart was generally a bad one for Sinatra. He spent the first six months fighting off allegations in connection with the "wrong door raid" — a bungled attempt to avenge friend Joe DiMaggio's wounded pride. The incident had taken place three years before, in 1954, and the legal issue still to be resolved was a question of conflicting testimonies. When Marilyn Monroe left DiMaggio, he was hurt and angry and reacted by hiring a pair of private detectives to keep tabs on her. When they reported that she was having a lesbian affair with a woman in an apartment house on Waring Avenue, he gathered together a group including Sinatra, Sanciola and the two detectives and raided the apartment. Unfortunately they smashed the wrong door down and found themselves in the home of a dazed neighbour. Sinatra claimed he waited in the car on the corner while the raid took place but one of the detectives said Sinatra was lying. The detective claimed to have been terrified to testify against Sinatra

Torn between Kim Novak and Rita Hayworth in 'Pal Joey'. It had been a hit for Gene Kelly on the stage, and was said to be unfilmable.

Sinatra produced and starred in 'Johnny Concho', a disappointing western.

Familiar faces at a benefit for Sammy Davis Jr: Jack Benny, George Burns, Sinatra and a youthful Mr and Mrs Reagan.

Sinatra chairing a tribute to heavyweight champ Joe Louis.

originally because of "rumours", later reinforced when he was beaten up. Eventually the neighbour settled out of court and the perjury charge could not be made to stick.

Next it was Sinatra's turn to sue. He objected so strongly to a "warts and all" profile in *Look* magazine that he tried to sue for huge libel damages. The first instalment, titled "Talent, Tantrums and Torment", set out to dispel the myth of Sinatra's slum upbringing, saying instead that Sinatra was a spoilt only child and going on to describe him as "a neurotic, depressed and tormented person with suicidal tendencies and a libertine". Sinatra was particularly enraged by an anecdote describing his encounter with the Speaker of the House, Sam Rayburn, at a Democratic rally. Rayburn was said to have laid a friendly hand on Sinatra's arm to be told, "Take your hands off that suit, creep." Although Rayburn denied the incident, the author of the *Look* profile produced an eye-witness to verify his account. The articles gained credibility when the author was awarded the Benjamin Franklin prize for the best profile in an American magazine. After six months on the warpath Sinatra changed his charge from libel to invasion of privacy, hoping his case would set a legal precedent. "I have always maintained that any writer or publication has a right to discuss or criticize my professional activities," he declared, as have many celebrities since. "But I feel that an entertainer has a right to his privacy, and that his right should be just as inviolate as any other person's right of privacy." With press freedom under threat, *Look* refused to back down. The legal wrangling lasted for years until Sinatra finally dropped his charges in 1963.

Although he became almost obsessive in his hatred of certain journalists over the years, Sinatra has his supporters. In his biography, Robin Douglas-Home describes the pressure Sinatra was under. "On at least three occasions while I was with Sinatra, items appeared in the columns referring to something he was meant to have said or done the previous evening — annoying items that certainly did not show him in a favourable light. Yet I knew these items were not based on any fact whatsoever, as I had been with him on the evenings in question."

In his favour, Sinatra's defenders cite his spontaneous generosity as a friend. There are tales of the support he gave Bela Lugosi when he was hospitalized for drug addiction. Sammy Davis Jr wrote extensively in his autobiography of the help Sinatra gave him with his career at a time when blacks faced terrible racism in the entertainment world, as elsewhere. Sinatra was at Bogart's side in his final months and rushed to Davis's bedside after the crash in which he lost his eye, giving him the encouragement he needed to return to the stage. He turned over his Palm Springs home to actor Lee J. Cobb, a man he didn't even know well, when he was hit by a heart attack,

and when the owner of the Mocambo died in 1957, leaving his wife in debt, Sinatra donated all his earnings from a run of shows at the club, bailing her out and giving her late husband a magnificent funeral. In 1977 he flew former world heavyweight champion Joe Louis across the country and paid for the heart operation that saved his life, and flew coast to coast to help console and perform with his friend Phil Silvers after the death of his partner Rags Ragland. The list goes on, and Sinatra was never the one to make use of it.

Maybe it was because Sinatra had been there. He had hit rock bottom and come back up to the top of his profession. More likely, his generosity towards a chosen few was an integral part of his romanticized self-image: a protecting and benevolent *padrone* in the Sicilian tradition. On the down side of his self-image was his easily injured pride. He could be the best, most loyal friend, but once slighted could take years to mellow. More often he never forgave those who broke his unwritten rules. Sorry was not in his vocabulary. The Sinatra history is littered with corpses, friends who fell foul of his temper, never to return to favour. Sammy Davis was one of the lucky ones. After admitting to an interviewer that Sinatra occasionally "stepped on people", he was written out of their forthcoming film and banished from Sinatra's sight. Only when Davis apologized publicly after months in the cold did Sinatra take him back in. Most feuds ended in deadlock or violence. His closest friends were scared of his temper. Over the years he even incorporated his grudges into his stage banter, offending and embarrassing his most loyal fans. Columnist Dorothy Kilgallen became a regular target after writing about Sinatra's string of female conquests in 1956. "Doesn't this look like Dorothy Kilgallen's profile," he would ask cruelly from the stage of the Sands, holding up one of his car keys. He typically failed to deal with the issues behind his anger, stooping instead to highly personal attacks. He repeatedly handled himself badly under stress, tending to go on the attack, then afterwards throwing money or gifts at victims of his temper in place of an apology. "You've got to decide which Sinatra you're looking for," said one Hollywood producer familiar with his alter ego, "the one who knocks people down or the one who lifts people up."

Sinatra and baseball great Joe DiMaggio, a friend whose marital problems with actress Marilyn Monroe landed both men in deep water.

Sinatra photographed in his Mayfair flat during a visit to England.

Chapter Seven

A POLITICAL AFFAIR, 1957

Sinatra and Rat Pack pals outside the hotel in which Sinatra had a stake.

Embittered by the failure of his marriage to Ava, Sinatra's subsequent relationships were fraught with problems. It was through Humphrey Bogart that he met the beautiful young actress Lauren Bacall. Although Bogart and Sinatra could not have been more different, Sinatra became a close friend and found acceptance within Bogart's clique of friends and entertainers, the Holmby Hills Rat Pack. After Bogart's death, Sinatra took up the mantle as Pack leader. He also began stepping out with Bogart's widow, Lauren Bacall, who has since revealed in her autobiography that they planned to marry. When Bacall jumped the gun, however, and inadvertently leaked the story to the press, she was unceremoniously dumped. He didn't speak to her again for six years. She called him an emotional coward; he preferred not to discuss it.

Although the offstage Sinatra once again threatened to sour his professional success, his music career continued to soar. With his records selling in their millions, *Playboy,* the bible of swinging bachelors like Frank, voted him top male vocalist. He won *Metronome's* Mr Personality with a landslide, was voted top male singer in the *Down Beat* poll and shared singer of the year in Jazz with Billie Holiday. The following year, 1958, *Come Fly with Me* and *Only the Lonely* were the top two albums and "Witchcraft" entered the singles charts.

Television was another matter. His much-hyped ABC TV series, for which he had been paid an incredible $3 million, was an extremely expensive flop. The entire series was shot in only a few weeks and it showed. In the press it was described as disorganized, dull and banal, with sloppy production and no direction. Colleagues blamed Sinatra's usual arrogance and failure to take the work seriously. At his own insistence, he had been given complete artistic control and had no one to blame but himself when the series was cancelled after twenty-six weeks.

One of Sinatra's guests on the ill-fated series was buddy Dean Martin. Along with Jerry Lewis, Joey Bishop, Peter Lawford, Sammy Davis Jr and mascot Shirley MacLaine, Martin was a member of Sinatra's new boys club, sometimes known as the Clan or Sinatra's Rat Pack once the activities of the Ku Klux Klan made the use of 'Clan' too sensitive. Beyond a devotion to drinking, the new-look Rat Pack bore little resemblence to its predecessor. While Bogart's group of educated sophisticates, including actor David Niven, historian Nathaniel Benchley, agent "Swifty" Lazar, Judy Garland, husband Sid Luft, Jimmy van Heusen and, of course, Bacall, had a genuine anti-establishment edge, Sinatra's Pack were all opportunistic front. Nevertheless, the on-screen chemistry between Martin and Sinatra was apparent from the moment they teamed up for television even if it did rub many people up the wrong way. "They performed like a pair of adult jevenile delinquents" said the *Chicago Sun-Times*.

"Just an ordinary bunch of guys who get together once a year and take over the world," says Sammy Davis Jr of the Clan.

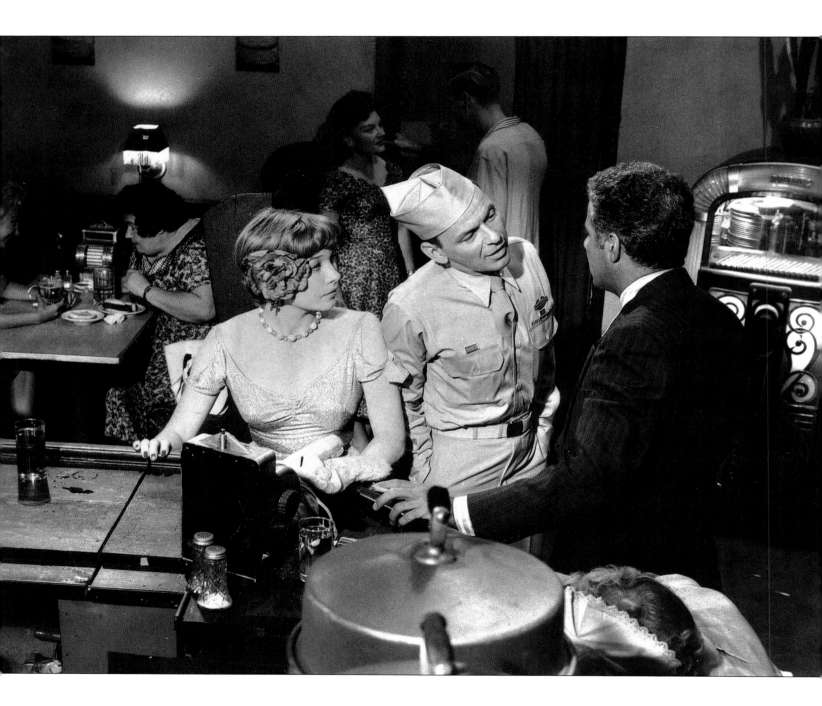

As the Fifties drew to a close, the films kept coming. *Kings Go Forth*, a rather glib tale of war, love and race with an improbably happy ending, was not one of Sinatra's best efforts. Slightly better was *Some Came Running*, a mean and moody melodrama in which he appeared with Clan mates Dean Martin and Shirley MacLaine. Next he starred in Frank Capra's comeback movie, *A Hole in the Head*. The critics were kind to the film which also did well at the box office and the jaunty *High Hopes* went on to win yet another Oscar for Cahn and Van Heusen. Capra found his own way of working with Sinatra, using improvisation to keep him fresh and getting a better performance than his previous few directors. He understood Sinatra well, saying, "The film set is torture for him. There's no audience." Other directors refused to take him on even if, like Billy Wilder, they felt he had "stupendous potential". Wilder blamed Sinatra's lack of concentration on his constant dabbling in a multitude of projects. Clan mascot and colleague Shirley MacLaine sugggested that by never giving everything to a film he had an escape route if it bombed. Instead of people saying he had failed, they would always say, "Just imagine what he could do if he really tried."

With Shirley MacLaine in 'Some Came Running', and alongside Tony Curtis in 'Kings Go Forth'.

In 1959 Sinatra made *Can Can* and *Never So Few*. His relationship with the press was terrible and predictions of his imminent downfall were widespread. The only person to benefit from *Never So Few* was newcomer Steve McQueen, previously a small-time TV actor, who won his role by default when Sinatra fell out with Sammy Davis Jr. The film marked McQueen's big breakthrough and set him on the road to superstardom. *Can Can*, based on a Cole Porter Broadway hit, was equally disappointing, but earned its place in Hollywood lore when Russian Premier Krushchev visited the set during a high-kicking chorus number and denounced the proceedings as immoral. The film also brought together Sinatra and co-star Juliet Prowse, to whom he became engaged a year or so later. It was a relaxed relationship, largely because Prowse left Sinatra to do the running, coolly ignoring his dalliances with, among others, Dorothy Provine, Marilyn Monroe and Princess Soraya. Their engagement ended after only six weeks, however, when Prowse refused to agree to Sinatra's precondition that she drop her career.

Sinatra offers a hand to Soviet Premiere Nikita Khrushchev on the set of 'Can Can'.

'Never So Few', the film that launched newcomer Steve McQueen.

ON THE SET WITH SINATRA

"Like your pleasure big? Come on in and find yourself a seat.

"We're on for Chesterfield every Friday night, ABC-TV.

"We've got music, drama, loads of stars!

"It all adds up to big, big pleasure . . .

like you get in Chesterfield.

"You can tell with one drag . . . You're smoking smooth—smoking clean!

"This is satisfaction—man-size satisfaction! Chesterfield!

"Ready to roll? Hold on. How can I do the show when this pack's empty!"

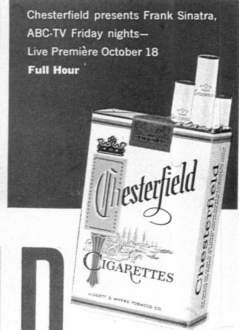

Chesterfield presents Frank Sinatra, ABC-TV Friday nights— Live Première October 18 **Full Hour**

CHESTERFIELD

KING and **REGULAR**

In 1960 ABC TV offered Sinatra another chance to prove himself on the small screen. Quite why is a mystery given his previous behaviour and ratings. This time they opted for a series of four specials, hoping to raise the quality and hold Sinatra's attention with the shorter run. To ABC's relief he fared better this time. The final show in particular shot up the ratings when he invited Elvis Presley as his guest. The occasion was ostensibly a "welcome home" party for Elvis, who had just finished military service. The motivation was clearly for Sinatra to bridge the generation gap and associate himself with whatever was currently cool.

The ploy may have worked temporarily, but the effect was short-lived. Sinatra had to accept that his appeal as a hipster was restricted to his own age group. He was now forty-five and attempts to prolong his youthful image through the Clan were a mistake. "To the young of the late 1950s and early '60s," wrote Derek Jewell, "very aware that something revolutionary was happening in *their* generation, the spectacle of these ageing heroes . . . indulging in jolly japes to extend the illusion of youth . . . must have been both bizarre and deterring."

The meeting of the generations: Sinatra with Elvis.

'Ocean's Eleven', one of the Rat Pack's better productions.

The first of the Clan movies, *Ocean's Eleven*, was the best of the bunch. All the gang were assembled — Frank and Dean, Sammy Davis Jr, Peter Lawford, Joey Bishop, female mascots Angie Dickinson and Shirley MacLaine, and token villain George Raft. Filming was a hoot and far from demanding, as each was basically required to play themselves. In the film, a traditional caper movie, Danny Ocean (Sinatra) summons ten old buddies from his commando days with the intention of simultaneously robbing five casinos on New Year's Eve. It was not a film to be taken seriously, but the in-crowd clowning was only mildly amusing and quickly wore thin in the subsequent spate of Clan movies.

By now Sinatra had built an impressive and diverse business empire with interests in most of his films, a number of publishing companies, substantial real-estate interests and casino stakes — six per cent in the Sands, Las Vegas, and twenty-five per cent in Cal-Neva, Lake Tahoe. Most important to Sinatra, though, was his newly formed independent recording company, Reprise. He had been released early from his Capitol contract and, on leaving, told the public to expect a "new, happier, emancipated Sinatra, untramelled, unfettered, unconfined". Initially Reprise lost money but it was only a matter of time before Sinatra turned things around.

With his burgeoning independence, certain sections of the press now began to portray Sinatra as a dangerously powerful man. Unfortunately, the image Sinatra projected with his violent outbursts and his position as "general" of the Clan did nothing to dispel the picture painted by the press. "Sinatra is King and Dictator of Hollywood," wrote the *New York Post*, "and everyone is afraid of him." As election year approached the right-wing attacks became more feverish.

The Sands Hotel earned Sinatra a lot of money, but was also the scene of many problems.

Sinatra with friend Peter Lawford and his wife Patricia Kennedy.

Sinatra with John F. Kennedy, a relationship certain to end in tears.

It was through fellow Clan member Peter Lawford that Sinatra gained entry to the most exclusive inner circle of them all, the Kennedy family. Lawford married Jack Kennedy's sister Patricia in 1954, immediately providing a bridge between the worlds of politics and show business. The young, handsome Kennedy was immediately drawn to the glamour of Hollywood and embarked on a series of affairs, starting with actress Gene Tierney. It was inevitable that Kennedy should team up with Sinatra. "Let's just say that the Kennedys are interested in the lively arts," said Lawford at the time, "and Sinatra is the liveliest art of all."

Sinatra's association with the Democrats was not new. But this time he had a more personal connection: the charismatic candidate was a man after his own heart — a lover of glamour, power and women. The relationship between the Kennedys and Sinatra was not dissimilar to Sinatra's relationship with that other family business, the Mob, based primarily on mutual backscratching. Sinatra gained kudos and to an extent realized his own political ambitions. Kennedy gained an influential and wealthy supporter, someone able and willing to drum up party funds and pull in the Italian Catholics while he took care of the Irish contingent. At a more human level, each allowed the other a glimpse into his world. But it would all end in tears.

From the moment Sinatra began to campaign for Kennedy there were those in the Democrat camp who worried about the damage Sinatra could do to the future President's image. There were Sinatra's gambling interests, the bad press, the shared sexual indiscretions, but above all the rumours of Mafia connections. But Sinatra's first *faux pas* was not at all what his critics might have expected. When the news broke in March 1960 that he was hiring Albert Maltz to adapt a novel for the screen, all hell broke loose. The right-wing press had been handed exactly what they wanted, a stick with which to beat the Kennedys and humiliate Sinatra. "Dump Maltz and get yourself a true American," threatened the *Los Angeles Examiner*. "If Sinatra loves his country he won't do this," whined Hedda Hopper melodramatically in the *Los Angeles Times*. John Wayne publicly demanded that Kennedy air his view on the hiring of a blacklisted "pinko" writer. A hysterical daily diatribe in the *Hollywood Reporter* condemned Sinatra as a "Commie apologist" and Maltz as a "sneaky, switchitting, strikebreaking FINK".

Many people forgot that Maltz had written the much-praised screenplay for Sinatra's first Oscar-winning film, *The House I Live In*. Since then, during the bad old days of McCarthyism, Maltz had been labelled a communist, one of the notorious "Hollywood Ten" who refused to testify before the House UnAmerican Activities Committee. He had also refused to name names. He was fined and imprisoned for a year, then like the others had been blacklisted, able to work only

Sinatra leads Jackie Kennedy, wife of the President elect, to her box at the pre-inaugural gala staged by Sinatra to help pay off the Kennedy campaign debt.

under an assumed name at low rates. To make matters worse the novel he was to adapt, *The Execution of Private Slovik*, was equally controversial. Slovik was the only soldier to have been executed by the American army since the end of the Civil War, not a potentially patriotic theme.

Sinatra initially stuck by Maltz, but despite his protestations that the screenplay would show that the army had been right and his reminder that the Bill of Rights guaranteed freedom of opinion, increasing pressure was brought to bear. Press rantings grew ever more vicious, drawing more and more people into the net, Clan members were dropped by advertisers, Steve McQueen's career was on the line (he was to play Slovik), the Catholic Church came out against him and it was made clear to Sinatra that he must disassociate himself either from Maltz or from Kennedy.

Eighteen days after the news broke, Sinatra collapsed under the pressure and issued a diplomatic press statement. "Due to the reactions of my family, friends and the American public, I have instructed my attorneys to make a settlement with Albert Maltz and to inform him that he will not write the screenplay of *The Execution of Private Slovik*. I had thought the major consideration was whether or not the resulting script would be in the best interests of the United States. Since my conversations with Mr Maltz had indicated that he had an affirmative, pro-American approach to the story, and since I felt fully capable as producer of enforcing such standards, I have defended my hiring of Mr Maltz. But the American public has indicated that it feels the morality of hiring Mr Maltz is the more crucial matter and I will accept the majority opinion."

As the election neared, the smears continued. Even Sammy Davis's impending marriage to May Britt, a white woman, was used against the Democrats, causing him to delay it until after the election. In the end Kennedy's popularity transcended the machinations of the press and, following his triumph at the polls, Sinatra was chosen to co-produce the inaugural gala with Peter Lawford, calling it "the most exciting assignment of my life". The star-studded event was an enormous success which finished with a personal thank you to Sinatra from Kennedy. "We are all indebted to a great friend," said JFK warmly, "Frank Sinatra. Tonight we have seen excellence."

Sinatra had survived this one, but in the long term his very public relationship with the President could not continue. When FBI and CIA files were opened in the 1970s as part of the post-Watergate investigation, the full extent of the problem was revealed. As early as 1960, Bobby Kennedy, soon to become Attorney General, had declared war on organized crime. Fearing his older brother's reputation could be compromised, one of his first moves was to investigate Sinatra's alleged *mafiosi* connections. Whatever Sinatra's "business" position, Bobby Kennedy found plenty to worry about. It was in 1960, for instance, that Jack Kennedy was introduced to one of Sinatra's former lovers, Judith Campbell-Exner. They were later to embark on an affair while at the same time she was sleeping with Public Enemy Number 1, Sam Giancana, and fellow Mobster John Roselli. Giancana reputedly controlled Chicago, the largest city in Illinois, the state that tipped the balance in Kennedy's favour when America went to the polls, and would later boast to Campnell-Exner, "Listen, honey, if it wasn't for me, your boyfriend wouldn't even be in the White House." FBI wiretaps from this period revealed countless compromising telephone calls in which Sinatra's name was often among those mentioned.

Bobby advised Jack to limit or end his friendship. The Campbell-Exner triangle was just one of Kennedy's more dangerous liaisons and the Marilyn Monroe connection another. In '62 Bobby delivered a cautious but damning report later made public by one of Sinatra's early biographers, Tony Scaduto. "Sinatra has had a long and wide association with hoodlums and racketeers," Bobby wrote to his brother, "which seems to be continuing. The nature of Sinatra's work may, on occasion, bring him into contact with underworld figures, but this cannot account for his friendship with and/or financial involvement with people such as Joe and Rocco Fischetti, cousins of Al Capone, Paul Emilio D'Amato, John Formosa and Sam Giancana . . . No other entertainer seems to be mentioned nearly as frequently with racketeers."

Eventually Jack Kennedy followed his prudent younger brother's advice. His friendship with Sinatra was quietly wound down. First a planned visit by Clan members to the President's villa at Cap d'Antibes in the summer of 1961 was cancelled, then came the final blow. While visiting Palm Springs in 1962, Kennedy was expected to stay at Sinatra's home, as he had done once before on the eve of the election. This time the delighted Sinatra had built a complete presidential wing with heliport and forty-seater dining room specifically for Kennedy's visit. It was like a public declaration of a love affair. Then, at the eleventh hour, the visit was cancelled. Giving security as as excuse, Kennedy went to stay instead with Bing Crosby. Peter Lawford was the unfortunate messenger. Sinatra, he claims, was livid. He initially refused to believe it could be true and then took a sledge hammer to the concrete heliport. He subsequently cut Lawford out of the forthcoming Clan movies and did not speak to him for many years. Sinatra had to blame someone for this great injustice but he couldn't bring himself to blame Kennedy. On the Maltz affair Sinatra had sacrificed his principles for Kennedy, he had publicly backed down — possibly for the first time — only to have the gesture thrown back in his face. Now, he had been betrayed a second time.

The end of the friendship signalled the end of Sinatra's links with the left.

He may have had political aspirations, he may have enjoyed the proximity to another kind of power, but, whatever his motives, he had worked extremely hard for Kennedy and put his heart as well as his time into the association. It was the end of an affair for Sinatra and led him to reject the politics learnt at his mother's knee, and pitch his tent with the Republicans.

It was inevitable that Bobby Kennedy's large-scale surveillance of key underworld figures should catch Sinatra in its net. It soon came to the attention of the Nevada State Gaming Board that Sinatra was entertaining known gangsters at the Cal-Neva Lodge. The Gaming Authority had banned certain Mobsters from state gambling premises. Giancana was on that list, but was found to have stayed at Cal-Neva with girlfriend Phyllis McGuire of the singing McGuire sisters. Under the threat of losing his licence, Sinatra was given two weeks to answer the charges against him. To everyone's surprise he decided not to fight, selling his gambling interests in both Cal-Neva and the Sands Casino. He held on only to his stake in the hotels, saying he wanted to limit his business interests to entertainment in future.

Much speculation followed this unexpected move. Some thought it was a last-ditch attempt to rekindle his relationship with Kennedy. He could not have known that Kennedy would be dead within three months. Others believed he bailed out just in time to avoid a potentially disastrous investigation. When Sinatra's son Frank Jr was kidnapped a few weeks after Kennedy's assassination, the rumours became ever wilder. He had been so horrified by Kennedy's assassination, suggested some, that he had decided to co-operate with Bobby and turn informer, and the kidnapping was a warning from the boys.

It can't have been easy for Frank Jr living in Sinatra's shadow. He had responded by modelling himself on his father. After launching his singing career that year, he was performing with ex-members of the Tommy Dorsey Band when he was snatched from his hotel room in Lake Tahoe. The ransom of $240,000 was paid and Frank Jr was returned unharmed. When the kidnappers were caught the next day and turned out to be amateurs, one of whom had been in school with Nancy Jr, a new rumour emerged — that the whole thing had been a publicity stunt by Frank Jr to kick-start his career. Although the hoax theory was dismissed by the judge, who doled out life sentences, the rumour persisted. Even when Sinatra successfully sued Independent Television for repeating the claim, his son's career and personal life were coloured by the accusation for many years.

Although this explanation has the least dramatic appeal, it's likely that Sinatra simply wanted to straighten out his business affairs. He was approaching fifty. With his best screen roles behind him and Reprise showing a profit, he may have seen himself

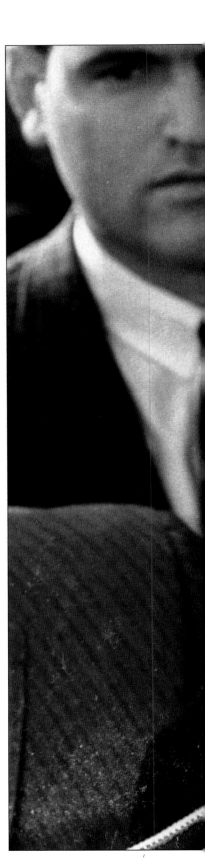

Frank Sinatra Jr, released by kidnappers after his father paid the 240,000 dollar ransom.

**The kidnapping was
surrounded by
rumours.**

becoming a full-time "businessman". A comment he made to Robin Douglas-Home a year earlier seems to confirm this: "As a singer I'll only have a few more years to go. As an actor maybe a few more than that, but not many. I've been performing out front for nearly thirty years now and frankly I'm getting a bit tired. Now, I want to do more and more behind the scenes, using my head."

CHAPTER EIGHT

A TIME FOR REFLECTION, 1962

Reprise was Sinatra's baby and he was certainly much more than a figurehead. He was deeply involved with all aspects of the business and the music it produced. In the early years Reprise was kept busy battling for ground against Capitol, but by 1962 Sinatra was outselling even Elvis, with fourteen albums on the bestseller list. The royalties from new and old recordings were more than enough to bail out Reprise. The label continued to blossom, eventually becoming so successful that Warner Brothers became interested in a merger. A lucrative deal was struck, leaving Sinatra with a third share, independence and a very tidy profit.

With Nelson Riddle tied to Capitol until 1963, Sinatra worked with a series of arrangers including Billy May, Sy Oliver, Don Costa and Count Basie's former arranger Neal Hefti. Free again, Riddle returned in '63 to collaborate on *The Concert Sinatra* and *Sinatra's Sinatra*. Both albums sold well, but critics noted that many of the older numbers previously recorded at Capitol lacked their old fire. Maybe it was a mistake to re-record these old favourites, but Sinatra no longer found it as easy to find the right material. This, plus a natural tendency to experiment, led to some of his less successful attempts at soft rock albums. Much better were his forays into jazz. He collaborated with Hefti and Basie to produce three fine jazz albums between 1961 and 1966, with *Sinatra-Basie* becoming an instant bestseller in 1963. He also went on to collaborate successfully with Duke Ellington and Brazilian bossa nova composer Antonio Carlos Jobim.

If some critics remained sniffy about Sinatra's contribution to jazz, musicians themselves were in no doubt. Both Duke Ellington and maverick Miles Davis have named him as their favourite singer and in 1965 a poll of jazz musicians voted Sinatra best-ever male vocalist for the second time, with fifty-nine votes to runner-up Nat King Cole's thirteen. Sinatra also had his champions amongst the press. After his historic perfomance with Basie at the Newport Jazz Festival, critic and biographer Arnold Shaw wrote that he had attended every festival since its inception, taking in the discoveries of

Sinatra and Dean Martin. Age did little to alter their adolescent antics.

geniuses Miles Davis in '55 and Dave Brubeck in '58, but that "no one individual had electrified and literally possessed the Festival as did Sinatra in 1965".

Sinatra did not fade away in the Sixties as he had predicted, but he did mellow with age. At fifty he was in reflective mood. It was the year that produced the single "It Was a Very Good Year", sensitively arranged by Gordon Jenkins, and an album with a similar theme, *September of My Years*. The single won two Grammys and the album one. In the same retrospective vein came *Sinatra: A Man and His Music* and, more surprisingly, a string of singles — "Strangers in the Night", "That's Life" and "Somethin' Stupid" (a duet with daughter Nancy) — which beat off the likes of the Beach Boys and the Beatles in a chart dominated by a new breed of musicians. Late in the Sixties came a series of autobiographical albums arranged by Don Costa — *Cycles, My Way* and *A Man Alone*. On these he made a brave if not always successful attempt to incorporate new material from singer-songwriters like Rod McKuen, Stevie Wonder and Joni Mitchell. Although patchy, *My Way* and *Cycles* both made gold albums, as did the anthology *Frank Sinatra's Greatest Hits*.

As was his norm, Sinatra juggled parallel careers in music, film, business and TV. It was no wonder, as he had admitted to Douglas-Home, that he felt tired. In the early Sixties he did a gruelling two-month tour of Mexico, Japan, Israel and Europe, donating over a million dollars to children's charities. This was written off by a cynical press as no more than an image-enhancing exercise. Whatever the motivation, his performances were applauded by ecstatic audiences. The *Financial Times* decribed his Festival Hall show as "85 minutes of

Sinatra's work with Count Basie and Basie's arranger Neal Hefti established him as a credible jazz singer – some said one of the best.

the most immaculate singing and entertainment" as "Sinatra glided effortlessly from song to song, mood to mood, tempo to tempo with impeccable assurance and poise. His voice was in superb condition," the enamoured critic continued, "and although practically every song was familiar, his unique phrasing imbued them with an almost alarming freshness . . ."

The films he made during these years ranged from poor to average: an indulgent guest spot as himself in the comedy *Pepe;* a heroic convict opposite Spencer Tracy's priest in *The Devil at Four O'Clock; Sergeants Three*, a misconceived attempt to take the Clan into 1870 Indian territory; and a bit part in one of Crosby and Hope's "Road" movies. He hadn't made a good movie since *Pal Joey* five years before, but things changed when *The Manchurian Candidate* came his way in 1962.

Sinatra not only co-starred in *The Manchurian Candidiate*, he was largely responsible for getting the film made. The novel by Richard Condon, a fast-moving conspiracy thriller, was put before Sinatra by director John Frankenheimer and screenwriter George Axelrod. He loved it and tried to sell the idea to United Artists, but they rejected it as politically sensitive: it was seen as anti-communist at a time when Kennedy was working on peace initiatives with Russia. Sinatra then appealed to the President himself, who agreed it would make a great movie and told Sinatra he was happy for him to go ahead. The film was completed in under forty days, a pace which suited Sinatra. After the private screening he described it as "the finest picture I have ever made".

The complex plot revolves around a group of American soldiers who are brainwashed while prisoners of war in Korea. They return home unaware that patrol leader Raymond Shaw (Laurence Harvey) has been programmed by the communists to respond to a predetermined trigger. At the sight of the Queen of Diamonds, he carries out a series of murders. His final mission is to assassinate the presidential nominee. It is Sinatra as his old buddy who guesses that something is amiss and sets off to pre-empt disaster. The slightly surreal scenes and endless twists which build to the dynamic climax are directed with flair and originality — some said too much originality when the film opened to confused audiences. In many ways the film was ahead of its time and didn't fit neatly into any established genre. It is part black comedy, part nail-biting thriller with an ambiguous political stance — it was picketed in Paris by the Communist Party, who saw it as American fascist propaganda, and by the American Legion in California, who said it was communist propaganda. Frankenheimer himself said the film was about the dangers of fanaticism, "the far left and the far right being exactly the same thing". But audiences were uncomfortable not knowing where they

"The only film I know that went from failure to classic without passing through success," said screenwriter George Axelrod of 'The Manchurian Candidate'.

stood or how they were expected to react. Noted American film critic Pauline Kael has called *The Manchurian Candidate* "the most sophisticated political satire ever made in Hollywood", but although some critics were generous, the box-office returns were not.

When Kennedy (who liked the film so much he kept his own private print) was assassinated a year later, the film took on a new resonance. It disappeared from circulation. Some said Sinatra had withdrawn it (he is also said to have withdrawn *Suddenly* after hearing Lee Harvey Oswald had watched the film shortly before the President was killed), others that United Artists had suppressed it. When it resurfaced many years later it achieved cult status with critics and audiences. "It was the only film I know," said George Axelrod,

"that went from failure to classic without passing through success."

Unfortunately the skill shown by Sinatra in championing *The Manchurian Candidate* did not continue. In 1963 he starred alongside Lee J. Cobb in *Come Blow Your Horn* and was one of a group of celebrities to take heavily disguised cameos in *The List of Adrian Messenger,* a weak whodunnit. A year later Frank and friends got together for yet another Clan movie, this time set in the wild west. It is often forgotten that the much-maligned Clan movies did well at the box office, something critics were reluctant to acknowledge. It was as if they felt the Clan made a mockery of film-making, something they took very seriously. As one critic wrote, "Sinatra worked so little that [Robert] Aldrich has more shots of the back of the head of Sinatra's

Sinatra on the set of 'Pepe', chatting with close friend Jack Entratter, once manager of the Copa and later the Sands Hotel.

'The Manchurian Candidate' – a commercial disaster but one of Sinatra's finest films.

COME FLY WITH ME... TO THE SANDS HOTEL!

Jet to Las Vegas in less than 5 hours flying time...from Anywhere, U.S.A. Come in pairs—singles—or crowds. Come where the finest in food, fanfare, and action flow around the clock; where every room and suite is the ultimate in luxury. Biggest shows, biggest stars, biggest time you'll ever have. The Sands IS relaxation...golf, swimming, horseback riding, boating or spectacular sightseeing. Climate, ideal! Oh yes! Come as you are! It's always casual and informal at the Sands Hotel. Now—venture that adventure you'll never forget...come jet with me to the Sands Hotel...Las Vegas. Where else!

FOR RESERVATIONS CALL: Chicago/CEntral 6-3317. Dallas/RIverside 2-6959. Las Vegas/DUdley 2-7100. Los Angeles/BRadshaw 2-8611. New York/PLaza 7-4454. Pittsburgh/EXpress 1-4028. San Francisco/EXbrook 7-2287. Toronto/EMpire 3-6728. **OR YOUR LOCAL TRAVEL AGENT.** Complete Convention Facilities including private meeting and dining rooms.

THE Sands

LAS VEGAS, NEVADA

double than he has of Sinatra." Maybe Sinatra picked up on this, because the Clan seemed to work harder on their next outing, *Robin and the Seven Hoods*, which transposed the Robin Hood legend to 1920s Chicago. The basic idea was a good one and the film produced a few memorable songs, including "My Kind of Town (Chicago Is)".

Next Sinatra was tempted to try the acting-directing double act with *None but the Brave*, and, like many before and since, he failed. The American Japanese co-production was a brave attempt to make an anti-war film, but Sinatra had missed the boat. Other films had already looked at America's role in the Second World War and made a better job of it.

It was on the set of his next film, Von Ryan's Express, that he met the woman who was to end his decade as a swinging bachelor, Mia Farrow. She was nineteen years old.

Born Maria de Lourdes Villers Farrow, Mia was the third of seven children of a first-generation Hollywood couple. Her mother, Maureen O'Sullivan, made over seventy films, but is best remembered as Jane to Johnny Weissmuller's Tarzan. Her father, the Australian John Farrow, was something of a renaissance man who started life as a research scientist turned writer and linguist, then headed for Hollywood and became a highly successful film director, often writing his own scripts. After converting to Catholicism he received several Papal honours for his series of distinguished religious biographies (which didn't prevent him establishing himself as a notorious ladies' man) and, as if his intellectual prowess were not enough, he was awarded a CBE for his bravery and leadership skills during the Second World War. After being invalided following a near-fatal attack of typhus, he returned to Hollywood to pick up an Academy Award for his screenplay for *Around the World in Eighty Days*.

John Farrow was clearly a somewhat overwhelming father figure, but also one who was absent for much of Mia's childhood. It is impossible not to link these factors with her attraction to older men, first Sinatra, over twice her age when they married, and later the conductor André Previn, sixteen years her senior.

Mia was seventeen when she got the acting bug, inevitable with her lineage, and within a year she had been spotted in an off-Broadway production of *The Importance of Being Earnest* and signed to Twentieth Century Fox for a five-picture deal. More significantly, she was picked to play Alison Mackenzie in a new ABC TV series called *Peyton Place*. The series débuted in 1964 and was the first real prime-time soap, the *Dallas* of its day; its stars became household names almost overnight.

There were very few things Mia could have done to raise her profile at this stage, but meeting and marrying Frank Sinatra was one

Sinatra was one of the hotel's biggest draws.

It was on the set of 'Von Ryan's Express' that Sinatra was romanced by his wife-to-be Mia Farrow.

Not exactly a match made in heaven, Farrow was around the same age as Sinatra's children.

'Von Ryan's Express'.

of them. "I want a big career, a big man and a big life," Mia told Hedda Hopper. "You have to think big." It was the deceptively frail and waiflike woman-child who pursued the older superstar, hanging around the set of *Von Ryan's Express* in a transparent dress until Sinatra could ignore her no longer.

"I liked him instantly," said Farrow. "He rings true. He is what he is." Sinatra's daughter Tina, not much older than Mia, took the relationship surprisingly well. In her biography of her father she described that first meeting: "Father told me Mia looked absolutely radiant. She was dressed in a sheer white dress and looked like an angel." Dolly, who still hoped for a reunion with Ava, dismissed her son's latest starlet. "She's a nice girl but that's all," she told the press. "My son is helping this girl to become a star." Mia's own mother was equally incredulous. "If Mr Sinatra is going to marry anyone," she said, "he ought to marry me."

An affair between the two certainly seemed unlikely. Sinatra in his custom-made suits, mixing it with the boys over traditional home-cooked pasta and Farrow, a Sixties girl, into mini-smocks, whole foods and meditation. She wanted a career. He wanted a wife and had made many press statements to this effect. "Somebody out of show business," he told *Life,* "or somebody who will get out." An unbeatable pair in terms of column inches, but hardly a recipe for marital bliss.

Against the odds they started seeing each other regularly, quickly becoming the subject of intense press interest and the fodder for topical jokes. Dean Martin joked that he had a Scotch older than Mia, while Eddie Fisher teased that Sinatra should buy her a teething ring rather than a wedding ring. Sinatra must have expected this kind of thing, but took exception to comedian Jacky Mason's harsher brand of humour. Mason ignored threats and public name-calling from Sinatra, making the couple a central part of his act. He joked about their bedtime rituals, Frank soaking his dentures while Mia brushed her braces, then peeling off his toupee while she undid her plaits. After the comedian ignored anonymous phone calls which demanded he drop the references to Frank and Mia, a gunman fired three shots into his Miami hotel room. Shortly afterwards, he was badly beaten by an unidentified assailant. No connection with Sinatra was ever made, although speculation was rife. Mason continued to use the material until it was no longer topical.

In 1965 Sinatra chartered a superb $2,000-a-day yacht to sail Mia and a handful of close friends on a four-week cruise off the coast of New England. The press had a field day with the extravagant event, dubbed "the most closely watched voyage since Cleopatra floated down the Nile to meet Mark Antony" by *Time* magazine. Reporters smelt marriage in the air and the writers of *Peyton Place*

were so sure the cruise would turn into a honeymoon that they wrote Mia's character into a coma.

Although retrospectively described as idyllic in Mia's autobiography, the relationship was not without its problems. The "haircut" affair was the most highly publicized of these. Mia's long blonde hair was an integral part of her angelic, little-girl look and when she decided to swap it for a tomboy crop without consulting Sinatra, the move didn't go down well. Her visit to Vidal Sassoon was supposedly a reaction to not being asked to Sinatra's enormous fiftieth birthday bash, organized by the two Nancys. Mia said she was simply bored with the old haircut, while her old friend Salvador Dali denounced it as "mythical suicide" and Ava quipped with characteristic wit, "I always knew Frank would wind up in bed with a boy." The fact that a haircut could cause such a kerfuffle gives some indication of the couple's celebrity at the time. Naturally, the "Mia" cut quickly became *de rigueur* among the smart young set.

Finally they married, amidst a blitz of flashbulbs at the Sands Hotel. It was the summer of 1966. Just over a year later they were divorced. The grounds cited were incompatibilty. Initially Mia had conformed to Sinatra's vision of married life. They stayed home, did crosswords, watched TV in bed and the only work she did was to redecorate their new Bel Air home. But the honeymoon period soon ended. Like Ava she had little time for the men she called his "nasty little chums". Even worse, and again like Ava, her career was about to peak — in Mia's case with *Rosemary's Baby*. Based on a book by Ira Levin and directed by Roman Polanski, the tale of satanic goings on in New York's famous Dakota Building was destined to become the most talked-about movie in town.

Frank and Mia married in 1966. "I finally found a broad I could cheat on," he joked four weeks later from the stage of the Sands.

Before and after the crop that launched a thousand haircuts.

**'Dirty Dingus Magee',
savaged by public
and press.**

**'Tony Rome' 1977. His
first appearance as a
private eye, a good
idea, but the film could
have been better.**

From the moment Mia accepted the part, her marriage was under threat. Sinatra issued an ultimatum, insisting she join him on the set of his latest film, *The Detective*, while she was still involved with putting the finishing touches to *Rosemary's Baby*. When Mia determinedly stayed put he contacted the studio direct and demanded they let her go. She wouldn't be bullied and didn't budge. Her decision was tantamount to requesting divorce papers and indeed they were delivered to her on the Paramount lot during filming only a few weeks later. Mia then took matters into her own hands, flying to Mexico on her first day off to process the papers herself. Independent to the last, she surprised everyone by leaving the marriage without demanding alimony or any assets. The press, the public and Sinatra had underestimated Mia Farrow.

Despite — or maybe because of — the emotional disruption during its making, *The Detective* was the first good film Sinatra had made since *The Manchurian Candidate*. Sadly, it was also his last good film. He plays the archetypal "honest cop" of the old school, surrounded by corruption and haunted by memories of his failed marriage. The lurid plot involves murder, mutilation, homosexuality and nymphomania, but amidst the high drama Sinatra puts in a beautifully understated performance as a disenchanted good guy. His film career was to go downhill from here, reaching rock bottom with the tacky spoof western *Dirty Dingus Magee* in 1970. "Disturbing and depressing beyond belief," wrote the New York Times, "to see this acute and awesome figure turning up time and time again in strangely tacky and trashy motion pictures." Sinatra's casting as a Chandleresque private eye in *Tony Rome* and *Lady in Cement* didn't live up to potential and the rest are barely worth a mention. His impeccable musical taste simply did not extend to film.

There was the violent but otherwise nondescript TV movie *Contract on Cherry Street,* then in 1980 his penultimate big-screen appearance in *The First Deadly Sin* in which he again plays a cop, this time on his final case. To finish he played himself (as did ageing playmates Dean Martin and Sammy Davis Jr) in *Cannonball Run II*, an unfunny car-chase movie of which *Variety* said, "This film is so inept that the best actor in it is Jilly Rizzo [Sinatra's real-life bodyguard]." It was a sad one to bow out on, unless you count his voice cameo for the cartoon character Singing Sword in *Who Killed Roger Rabbit* (1988), a far, far better film.

Sinatra was an instinctual actor whose best perfomances often came out of personal experience or emotional turmoil in his private life. His natural passion for music had to be generated elsewhere for a film to work. Although he had the gravitas and perhaps the ability to extend his film career into old age he lacked the motivation. One can't help wondering what kind of an actor he might have made if he hadn't had a voice.

CHAPTER NINE

DANCING IN THE DARK, 1970

Sinatra's swansong. "Hell, I just quit, that's all," he told reporters. "I don't want to put on any more make-up. I don't want to perform any more."

As the Sixties drew to a close, Sinatra was at a low ebb. His third marriage had ended and he was once again alone. It had been a busy, productive decade, but now, as the Seventies stretched before him, he complained about the dearth of good film scripts and music. He rejected most of the material that was put his way saying, "Nobody's writing any songs for me."

The Sixties closed sadly with the death of his father, Marty, a reminder of his own mortality which was compounded when he developed health problems in 1970. An operation for Dupuyten's Contracture, which distorts palm and fingers, alleviated but could not cure the condition affecting his famous microphone hand. Speculation about his health grew alongside press murmurs of retirement. But when Sinatra did announce his retirement in March 1971, friends and fans were shocked. He was seen as a survivor, not a quitter. The announcement said that although he considered himself lucky to have enjoyed three decades that had been "fruitful, busy, uptight, loose, sometimes boisterous, occasionally sad, but always exciting", there had been "little room or opportunity for reflection, reading, self-examination and that need which every thinking man has for a fallow period, a long pause in which to seek a better understanding of changes occurring in the world. This seems a proper time to take that breather," he concluded.

His farewell performance took place at the Los Angeles Music Centre, on 14 June 1971. Columnist and biographer Earl Wilson called the historic event "an epic evening of epic evenings". His evocative description of Sinatra's final number, "Angel Eyes", recalls a poignant exit: "He asked for the stage to be darkened, just a pinpoint spot on him. Midway through the song, he lit a cigarette. The smoke wrapped him within it. He was in silhouette. He came to the last line of the song, *excuse me while I disappear*. And he did."

It was seen as the end of an era. Benny Green, musician and *Observer* jazz critic at the time, said on Sinatra's retirement, "What

Sinatra relaxes with
Vice-President Spiro
Agnew, and lends a
hand to President Nixon
at a White House State
dinner for the Italian
Prime Minister.

few people apart from musicians have ever seemed to grasp is that he is not simply the best popular singer of his generation, but the culminating point in an evolutionary process which has refined the art of interpreting words set to music. Nor is there ever the remotest possibility that he will have a successor. Sinatra was the result of a fusing of a set of historical events which can never be repeated."

It didn't take long for Sinatra to fulfil his need for "a fallow period". Life in Palm Springs was certainly comfortable, but maybe a tad too comfortable for a man who had spent most of his life in the centre of the action. He may have hated with a passion the all-seeing eye of the press, but at the same time his public persona was an integral part of his identity. Performance was a vital outlet for his high energy levels and in time he found he couldn't do without it. Ignoring the old adage "quit while you're ahead", he returned to public performance in 1973.

The intervening years had been quiet, allowing him to recharge his batteries. He still made headlines occasionally. In '72 he made mincemeat of the House Select Committee on Crime when accused and cleared of involvement with illegal goings-on at a Massachusetts racecourse. He also made news when Barbara Marx left her husband Zeppo and moved in with him. The former show girl with her very American brand of blonde, Barbie-doll beauty was the perfect hostess and the ideal partner for Sinatra. She may have lacked the star status of her two most recent predecessors, but she also lacked their career drive and independence. She had ambition all right, but of a different kind: her aim was to marry well. In Sinatra's case this meant biding her time.

As Sinatra's relationship with Barbara grew so did his friendship with Spiro Agnew, Republican Governor of Maryland when they met and Vice-President to Richard Nixon a few years later. Sinatra's switch to the right provoked mixed reactions. Some attributed it solely to his snub from the Kennedys, while others saw it as a natural function of ageing. It's certainly not uncommon for self-made men like Sinatra to turn on a new generation they see as having it too easy and to become protective about the material wealth they have worked so hard to acquire. Others, like critic and former Sinatra supporter Ralph Gleason, could never forgive a turncoat. "The voice is good today," he wrote in *Rolling Stone* magazine, "but I don't believe any more that he is one of us. He's one of them now, singing from the other side of the street." What dyed-in-the-wool Democrat Dolly thought did not make it into print, although an incongruous photo shows her proudly being introduced to Agnew.

Sinatra went on to support Ronald Reagan's 1970 gubernatorial campaign in California, particularly taken with his confrontational stand against student demonstrations, then went on

Barbara Marx, in many
ways the perfect wife
for Sinatra.

Barbara and Frank Sinatra
California

The most unforgettable women   in the world wear REVLON

Barbara is wearing Revlon Nail Enamel and Super Lustrous™ Lipstick in Revlon Red.   © 1989 Revlon, Inc.

to offer his campaigning services to Republican presidential candidate Richard Nixon.

Sinatra once again had friends in the White House. He needed to be on his best behaviour, but Mafia rumours continued to feed his hatred of the press and when he bumped into Maxine Chesire, a *Washington Post* reporter who had recently written on the subject, his anger boiled over into an extremely ugly confrontation. Chesire made the mistake of approaching Barbara Marx at a private pre-inaugural party and Sinatra lost control. His words of abuse were widely reported and if anything toned down. "Get away from me you scum," he ranted. "Go home and take a bath. I'm getting out of here to get rid of the the stench of Miss Chesire . . . You're nothing but a two dollar whore . . . you've been laying down for two dollars all your life. Here's two dollars, baby," he concluded, stuffing the bills into her drink, "that's what you're used to." He didn't stop there, but the rest of his tirade was considered unprintable. Incredibly, Nixon was unphased and invited Sinatra to sing at the White House only a few months later in honour of the Italian Prime Minister. His subsequent words of appreciation were such that Sinatra was moved to tears. Such a captivating and magical talent, said Nixon, should not be confined to the select few. And so the comeback began.

This personal invitation to return from retirement was assumed by some to have political as well as musical implications. If so,

Acceptance at the White House once again.

Sinatra was once again out of luck. Within a few weeks Watergate, the biggest political scandal in recent American history, had burst wide open. "Did you ever think you would see a time when Frank Sinatra would be ashamed to be seen with a President of the United States?" quipped Ethel Kennedy, Bobby's widow. Soon after, Spiro Agnew was also discredited for financial mismanagement during his governorship of Maryland and resigned, despite Sinatra's loyal if misguided attempts to have his friend reinstated. Although accused at one stage of having been on the receiving end of tax favours allegedly meted out by Nixon to close friends, Sinatra was cleared and emerged unscathed.

In early 1973 Sinatra had recorded a batch of songs later released as his comeback album *Ol' Blue Eyes is Back*. He was back doing what he knew best and, as always, his emotional life was reflected in carefully selected numbers like "Let Me Try Again" and "Send in the Clowns". At the time of the album's release Sinatra was buoyed up by an award from the Songwriters of America — Entertainer of the Century — and in November his official "retirement from retirement" was marked by an hour-long NBC special. Named for the album, the show took place in front of a specially invited black-tie audience and despite Sinatra's occasional vocal lapses, critics and fans were delighted with what they heard. Even watching that special on video today it is impossible not to to be moved by Sinatra.

President Nixon begged Sinatra to come back – and he did.

By the end of 1973 Ol' Blue Eyes was back, and in fighting form on and off stage.

1974 found him at the centre of a full scale battle with the Australian media. Legal advisor Milt Ruden (centre with arms folded) faced the music on Sinatra's behalf.

His voice is still much better than it should be for a man his age and that comes from within. He sings classics he has performed hundreds of times, but with renewed emotion and conviction. There is nothing half-hearted about Sinatra's performance and the audience can't help but rise to meet his involvement.

Seemingly unable to adopt any other pace, Sinatra launched himself once again into a frenetic schedule that would have been gruelling for a man half his age. By the time 1974 came around he was performing live at Caesar's Palace and packing them in at Carnegie Hall just like the old days. A trade press advertisement he took out in 1975 boasted that he had played 140 dates in 105 days. After releasing another album, *Some Nice Things I've Missed*, he set off to tour Japan, the Middle East and finally Australia, where the less desirable elements of Ol' Blue Eyes resurfaced.

On arrival in Australia, Sinatra was pestered by reporters keen to interview him. Tired and angry, he turned the situation over to his bodyguards and a minor scuffle ensued. Sinatra was quoted as calling the Australian press "bums, parasites, hookers and pimps". As was becoming increasingly common, he singled out the women for particularly unpleasant abuse. "They are the hookers of the press," ran the usual tirade. "I might offer them a buck and a half. I once paid a broad in Washington two dollars," he went on, referring to the Maxine Chesire incident. "I overpaid her, I found out. She didn't even bathe — most of them don't." Australia was shocked by the behaviour and language of a man they had been prepared to welcome as a legend. When Sinatra demanded apologies from the Australian Journalists' Association, the Transport Workers' Union responded by boycotting him. Sinatra was a prisoner, unable to refuel his private plane and barred from buying an ordinary ticket. Following a heartfelt and diplomatic appeal by Bob Hawke, then head of the Australian Council of Trade Unions and a Sinatra fan himself, both sides muttered carefully worded half-apologies reeking of insincerity. The tour ground on amid jibes, bad press and bad behaviour.

Within weeks of his return to the States Sinatra was under scrutiny once again, when businessman Frank Weinstock accused him of ordering his bodyguards to rough him up in the men's room of a Palm Springs hotel in 1973. After accusing Weinstock of making eyes at his wife, Sinatra had allegedly pushed Weinstock, then stood back and let his men finish the job. Sinatra was eventually cleared but Jilly Rizzo was charged with assault and battery.

Sinatra's reputation for socializing with criminals took on a new feel now as Watergate prompted America to acknowledge corruption at all levels. There was renewed contempt for those who abused positions of power and respect. In *Rolling Stone*, former supporter Ralph Gleason ridiculed Sinatra's image, calling him "an arrogant

Only a few years later Sinatra appeared in court to deny rumours of Mafia ties. Legally he was vindicated but the story refused to die.

Sinatra with his mother, Dolly, the most influential woman in his life, and Ava, the runner up, and Mia.

Friends and colleagues gather to honour Sinatra as he is presented with the Pied Piper award of The American Society of Composers, Authors and Publishers by friend and songwriter Jules Styne. Also present, (from left to right) Paul Anka, Milton Berle, Glen Ford, Rich Little, Harry James, Sammy Cahn, Dionne Warwick and Henry Mancini.

despot" surrounded by "a court of sycophants". In the *Boston Globe*, George Frazier wrote, "The trouble with you, Frankie, is you got no style. All your life you wanted to be a big man but the wrong kind of big man. Look, Sinatra, Momo Giancana is just another version of Haldeman, and Agnew makes three. You're a sad case, Frankie. I think you're the best male vocalist who ever lived, but I also think you're a miserable failure as a human being."

These words must have hurt. They hit the nail on the head and they did it in Sinatra's language. Once the public began to see Sinatra as part of the newly discovered national rot, they were cynical about every move he made: shows of generosity were interpreted as ego trips, charity work as attempts to rehabilitate his image.

Touring in the mid Seventies was fraught with problems. Not for the first time London offered a peaceful and appreciative stop off. Two shows at the Albert Hall went down well, the first of which boasted an audience that included two ex-wives (Gardner and Farrow) and three princesses — Margaret, Anne and Grace of Monaco. Despite complaints about ticket prices, the shows were heavily oversubscribed and touts made a killing selling £30 seats for over £250. There followed a series of shows with singer-songwriter of the moment John Denver, and a successful two-week run at the Uris Theatre, New York, sharing the bill with Ella Fitzgerald and Count Basie. To end the run Jackie Onassis was snapped escorting

Sinatra to the theatre. She was reportedly trying to sign him up for a autobiography on behalf of a New York publisher, but whatever the reason, Sinatra basked in the glow of acceptance, if only by Kennedy's widow. He followed this with an equally successful run at the London Palladium with Basie and Sarah Vaughan, this time with Spiro Agnew joining him to celebrate his triumph. In a profile for the *Evening Standard* Ray Connolly attempted to explain Sinatra's presence, pointing to the actor in him: "He sings as he moves, gently foxtrotting from side to side, snapping his white cuffs to add interpretation, briskness and style, then sloping down his shoulders into that thin-man look of lost love and instant vulnerability. From a lesser performer such theatricals might have been embarrassing, but he's so subtle that one cannot fail to join in the mood."

In May 1976 Barbara's patience was rewarded. The bride gave the groom a Jaguar XJS and he returned the gesture with a gleaming Rolls Royce. Although Sinatra returned to work within two days of the happy event he did slow down over the following year with shorter runs in a more selective venues. "I really have found a new kind of tranquillity," he said.

At this stage in Sinatra's life the death of his mother was inevitable, but when it happened it felled him like a tree. At eighty-two she still seemed as indestructible, as indomitable as she had been when Sinatra was a teenager. Dolly was on her way to

see Sinatra perform in Las Vegas when the private plane in which she was travelling disappeared shortly after leaving Palm Springs. It took days before the bodies were recovered from the snowy wilderness of the San Bernadino mountains.

Proud and supportive, Dolly was a powerful figure in Sinatra's life right to the end. As a domineering figure, emotionally absent for much of his childhood, she was certainly a key force behind his relentless drive to succeed in his own right and on his own terms.

Whether as a result of his marriage, the loss of his mother or age, Sinatra quietened down during the second half of the Seventies. He tried to keep out of the headlines not only by staying out of trouble but by barricading himself in behind the security fences and fleets of heavies at his fortress-like home. As he turned inwards, the press responded by writing with contempt of his tightly sealed, self-made world. It was around this time, in the late Seventies and early Eighties, that the Sinatra image began to take over from the performer. His original audience were now in their sixties and the new generation of record buyers and concert-goers, without their own memories to fall back on, had only the Sinatra myths to go on.

In 1981 the one-time anti-racism campaigner did his image no good when he agreed to perform in Sun City, South Africa, for a fee in excess of £1 million. This was followed by his battle to stop writer Kitty Kelly publishing a sensational unauthorized biography. Sinatra unwittingly played right into her hands by generating so much publicity that the book was a guaranteed bestseller before it was written. He began by circulating a letter to anyone she might conceivably contact warning that they co-operated at their peril. He then cranked up the mighty legal machinery at his disposal and set it in motion against Kelly, while at the same time using the press to

issue threats against her. He claimed she was misrepresenting herself to his friends and that only his company had the right to exploit his name and image. As so often before he overdid it, enraging in the process the National Writers' Union and the American Society of Journalists and Authors, for whom the issue became a question of press freedom. Ever canny, Kitty Kelly played her part. When asked what she was being paid for her research, she replied, "A million dollars plus a choice of funeral gown to be laid out in."

As the battle dragged on it became clear that Sinatra had rubbed the world's press the wrong way and could not win this one. His next ploy was an attempt at a spoiler of his own. In 1984 he announced he would collaborate with his daughter Tina on a "warts and all" TV mini-series of his life. When the promised mini-series was eventually broadcast it was doomed to disappoint in the wake of the Kelly exposé. As expected, it was selective, and while it was surprisingly open about some aspects of Sinatra's life — drinking, depression, infidelity — it left other myths undisturbed. The Kelly biography was an enormous moneyspinner and made compulsive reading, but in its own way also left a lot out, concentrating on Sinatra's personality at the expense of his talent.

In 1980 Sinatra released *Trilogy*, a three-album set which formed an overview of his career. The three parts "Past", "Present" and "Future" each have their own arranger, Billy May, Don Costa and Gordon Jenkins, and take the listener on a journey beginning with a new version of his first song, "The Song is You" and building to a full-blown orchestral finale with "Before the Music Ends". It was his first album for five years, and critic Derek Jewell felt the years had added to Sinatra's performance: "The uncertainties in Sinatra's voice, the tension as one wondered if he would *quite* make a note or a leap,

Sinatra's home in Los Angeles, a luxurious fortress.

gave an extra edge of poignancy to his ballads, like 'More Than You Know', a classic example of art overcoming age and ability".

Sinatra continued to tour, frequently making large charitable donations along the way. In 1984 England awaited his first visit since 1980 when he had promised to return to the venue he had made his own, the Royal Albert Hall. In the event, he arrived under a cloud. When a downpour hit his open-air show in Toronto he sang for only twenty-five minutes, leaving behind him an angry mob who had paid around $75 a head for the privilege. Then, on the eve of his departure for London his name hit the headlines in connection with a new book by "Mafia Princess" Antoinette Giancana, daughter of the notorious Mobster. Pre-publication publicity trumpeted that the FBI now held a file on Sinatra weighing fourteen pounds.

Sinatra arrived in London in aggressive mood, surrounded by bully boys and mouthing "the Francis Albert hall" like a heavyweight boxer psyching himself up for a fight. His behaviour alienated fans and irritated journalists. It is clear from the mixed reviews that

Bad press and a failing voice never affected the fans.

Sinatra's voice, filtered through a range of preconceptions and emotions from deaf loyalty to blind contempt, could no longer be assessed objectively. People heard what they wanted to hear. For die-hard fans, simply being there was enough. The new generation of tabloid writers, however, revelled in the downfall of a sacred cow and went for the kill; "a bloated old-age pensioner", "sewn, patched and thatched", not a "crooner" but a "croaker", "the magic is gone". Sinatra's great saviour from the broadsheets, Derek Jewell, was in hospital at the time of the Albert Hall performances. A few years before he had written joyfully in the *Sunday Times* of Sinatra the ageing performer: "See how he enjoys his work. Sinatra responds to, loves, gets a kick from every nuance of beat and colour in the music. He's just knocked out by a good orchestration, is transformed by it. No wonder he performs popular songs so well. No wonder he couldn't stay retired. He lives, I conclude, for music. And the music lives for him." He found it hard to accept the new, harsh reviews, citing Sinatra's latest album, *LA Is My Lady,* as evidence of the singer's unique ability to transcend his diminishing vocal skills. For the album Sinatra had assembled a fine team headed by Quincy Jones and featuring musicians as diverse as George Benson and Lionel Hampton

to cover songs as wide-ranging as "Mack the Knife" and the new title number. That same year Sinatra fans were delighted with the reissue of sixteen classic 1950s albums from the glorious Capitol years.

A year later, in 1985, Sinatra was again at the side of Ronald Reagan, this time on the occasion of his second inaugural gala. This made him a target for the press and the old allegations were hauled out once again. Sinatra took it as badly as ever and in one embarrassing outburst shouted to reporters, "You're dead, every one of you. You're dead." This could have been a problem for Reagan, who had been called upon to defend Sinatra against similar allegations only a few years earlier. Then he had responded with a letter of support (later auctioned for a record price of $12,000). "I have known Frank Sinatra for a number of years," he wrote. "I am aware of the incidents, highly publicized quarrels with photographers, night club scrapes etc, and I admit it is not a lifestyle I emulate or approve. However, there is a less publicized side to Mr Sinatra which justice must recognize. I know of no one who has done more in the field of charity than Frank Sinatra." This time around Reagan surprised most and outraged many Americans by presenting Sinatra with the Medal of Freedom at the White House.

President Reagan awards Sinatra with the Presidential Medal of Freedom, 1985. Some years later the press would speculate about Sinatra's "special relationship" with the First Lady.

Sinatra performing at the inaugural gala for President elect Ronald Reagan.

Chapter Ten

FINALE, 1985

The last decade has been a quiet one, hardly surprisingly for a man approaching eighty, even for a man like Sinatra. His only new recordings from this period are the *Duets* albums from 1993 and 1994, on which he covers a selection of old favourites with an incongruous collection of singers including Aretha Franklin, Gloria Estefan, Charles Aznavour, Linda Ronstadt, Gladys Knight and U2's Bono, the most misconceived of all the pairings. Thanks to the miracle of modern technology, the duets were recorded in a way which doesn't require participants to be in the same city, let alone the same studio. They have a smooth professionalism but a strangely hollow ring and although some, like "In the Wee Small Hours" with Carly Simon, will still move the emotional to tears, so would the 1955 original. The albums are not so much bad as redundant. Nevertheless, advance orders for *Duets I* topped 1 million; it went straight into the British top ten and eventually sold over 5 million copies worldwide. Following in its footsteps, *Duets II* went Gold (100,000 copies) within a month of release.

Still performing public duties as well as professional bookings.

He still performs, of course. The last time he appeared at the Royal Albert Hall was 1989, but in 1990 he filled the Wembley Arena and was still able to mesmerize the crowds. Although he wowed them with an hour-long set at the Coliseum as recently as 1992, still rolling out the imaginary dice as he pounced on "Luck be a Lady", his shows tend to be only for the most forgiving fans nowadays, with Sinatra dependent on an autocue, still losing the lyric on occasions. Celebrity-watchers say he is suffering from symptoms associated with Alzheimer's disease. After seeing him perform in 1994 at the Omni Centre, Atlanta, Richard Williams wrote in the *Independent*, "His thoughts seem adrift . . . He was performing not from memory but from the reserves of some deeper faculty, a reflex conditioned by decades of stages and microphones and footlights." Yet when Sinatra closed the show with the same old moves and props — the lonely barstool, the smoking cigarette — and moved into a tender rendition of "Guess I'll Hang My Tears Out to Dry", Williams too was transported, along with the weeping women whose children were likely conceived to the strains of a young Sinatra.

The presence of a
legend for the grand
reopening of
Carnegie Hall.

**Reunited with the
Rat Pack.**

He still makes headlines for all the wrong reasons. In 1991 he was accused of cuckolding President Reagan and in 1993 he featured in the tabloids when a Surrey housewife revealed herself as the "secret daughter" of Ol' Blue Eyes, the result of an affair with actress Eva Bartok thirty-seven years earlier. The past just won't let Sinatra go. A few months before he had been at the centre of a different kind of controversy. After receiving a special lifetime acheivement award at Radio City Music Hall, he began to speak, slowly and falteringly. A few minutes into his confused discourse the director of CBS's live telecast unceremoniously cut him off and moved to an ad break. Following an uproar, CBS apologized. Days later fans held their breath when Sinatra was carried from the stage in Richmond, Virginia, halfway through a performance of "My Way". It seemed a perfect if tragic exit. Sinatra was clearly not ready to bow out, however, and discharged himself from hospital hours later, returning to his Palm Springs home to recover from dehydration brought about by the high temperatures in the auditorium.

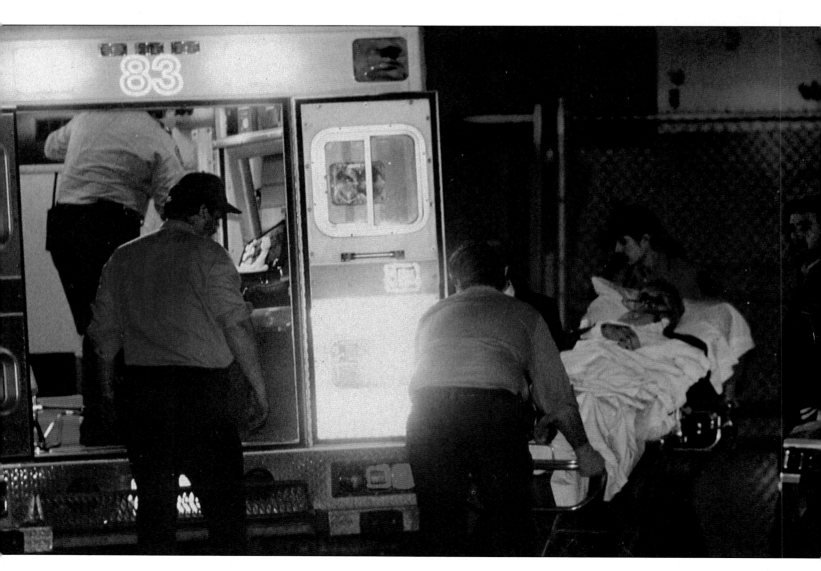

At the time of writing Sinatra is still touring and audiences are queuing to see him, which begs the obvious question — why does he do it? The answer is that performing is simply what Sinatra does, what he is. And if only a few minutes of an overblown two-hour concert reveal an echo of the original magic, why should he stop?

BIBLIOGRAPHY

Bacall, Lauren
By Myself
Alfred Knopf, 1979

Davis Jr, Sammy; Boyar, Jane and Burt
Yes I Can: The Story of Sammy Davis Junior
New York Pocket Books, 1966

Douglas-Home, Robin
Sinatra
Grosset and Dunlap, 1962

Gardner, Ava
Ava: My Story
Bantam Press, 1990

Howlett, John
Frank Sinatra
Plexus Publishing, 1980

Jewell, Derek
Frank Sinatra: A Celebration
Pavilion, 1985

Kelly, Kitty
His Way: The Unauthorized Biography of Frank Sinatra
Bantam Press,1986

Pickard, Roy
Frank Sinatra at the Movies
Robert Hale, 1994

Ringgold, Gene
The Films of Frank Sinatra
Citadel, 1989

Rockwell, John
Sinatra: An American Classic
Rolling Stone Press, 1984

Rubin, Sam; Taylor, Richard
Mia Farrow
Robson Books, 1989

Wilson, Earl
Sinatra: An Unauthorized Biography
Atheneum, 1961

FILMOGRAPHY

Las Vegas Nights, 1941
Director: Ralph Murphy
Cast: Constance Moore, Bert Wheeler, Tommy Dorsey and his Orchestra with Frank Sinatra on vocals

Ship Ahoy, 1942
Director: Jack Cummings
Cast: Eleanor Powell, Red Skelton, Tommy Dorsey and his Orchestra with Frank Sinatra on vocals

Reveille with Beverley, 1943
Director: Charles Barton
Cast: Ann Miller, William Wright, Dick Purcell and featuring Frank Sinatra

Higher and Higher, 1943
Director: Tim Whelan
Cast: Michele Morgan, Jack Haley and Frank Sinatra

Step Lively, 1944
Director: Tim Whelan
Cast: Frank Sinatra, George Murphy, Gloria DeHaven

Anchors Aweigh, 1945
Director: George Sidney
Cast: Frank Sinatra, Kathryn Grayson, Gene Kelly

The House I Live In, 1945
Director: Mervyn LeRoy
Cast: Frank Sinatra

Till the Clouds Roll By, 1946
Director: Richard Whorf
Cast: June Allyson, Lucille Bremer, Judy Garland, Kathryn Grayson, Lena Horne, Van Heflin and guest star Frank Sinatra

It Happened in Brooklyn, 1947
Director: Richard Whorf
Cast: Frank Sinatra, Kathryn Grayson, Peter Lawford, Jimmy Durante

The Miracle of the Bells, 1948
Director: Irving Pichel
Cast: Fred MacMurray, Alida Valli, Frank Sinatra, Lee J. Cobb

The Kissing Bandit, 1948
Director: Laslo Benedek
Cast: Frank Sinatra, Kathryn Grayson

Take Me Out to the Ball Game, 1949
Director: Busby Berkeley
Cast: Frank Sinatra, Gene Kelly, Esther Williams, Jules Munshin, Betty Garrett

On the Town, 1949
Directors: Gene Kelly and Stanley Donen
Cast: Gene Kelly, Frank Sinatra, Betty Garrett, Ann Miller

Double Dynamite, 1951
Director: Irving Cummings
Cast: Jane Russell, Groucho Marx,Frank Sinatra

Meet Danny Wilson, 1951
Director: Joseph Pevney
Cast: Frank Sinatra, Shelley Winters, Alex Nichol

From Here to Eternity, 1953
Director: Fred Zinnemann
Cast: Burt Lancaster, Montgomery Clift, Deborah Kerr, Donna Reed, Frank Sinatra, Ernest Borgnine

Suddenly, 1954
Director: Lewis Allen
Cast: Frank Sinatra, Sterling Hayden, James Gleason

Young at Heart, 1955
Director: Gordon Douglas
Cast: Doris Day, Frank Sinatra, Gig Young, Ethel Barrymore

Not as a Stranger, 1955
Director: Stanley Kramer
Cast: Olivia de Havilland, Robert Mitchum, Frank Sinatra, Gloria Grahame

The Tender Trap, 1955
Director: Charles Walters
Cast: Frank Sinatra, Debbie Reynolds, Celeste Holm, David Wayne

Guys and Dolls, 1955
Director: Joseph L. Mankiewicz
Cast: Marlon Brando, Frank Sinatra, Jean Simmons, Vivian Blaine

The Man with the Golden Arm, 1955
Director: Otto Preminger
Cast: Frank Sinatra, Eleanor Parker, Kim Novak

Meet Me in Las Vegas, 1956
Director: Roy Rowland
Cast: Dan Dailey, Cyd Charisse, Jerry Colonna, Lena Horne and Frank Sinatra as unbilled guest star

Johnny Concho, 1956
Director: Don McGuire
Cast: Frank Sinatra (also producer), Keenan Wynn, Phyllis Kirk

High Society, 1956
Director: Charles Walters
Cast: Bing Crosby, Grace Kelly, Frank Sinatra, Celeste Holm

Around the World in Eighty Days, 1956
Director: Michael Anderson
Cast: David Niven, Cantinflas, Shirley MacLaine, Robert Newton and cameo appearance by Frank Sinatra

The Pride and the Passion, 1957
Director: Stanley Kramer
Cast: Cary Grant, Frank Sinatra, Sophia Loren

The Joker is Wild, 1957
Director: Charles Vidor
Cast: Frank Sinatra, Mitzi Gaynor, Jeanne Crain, Eddie Albert

Pal Joey, 1957
Director: George Sidney
Cast: Rita Hayworth, Frank Sinatra, Kim Novak

Some Came Running, 1958
Director: Vincente Minelli
Cast: Frank Sinatra, Dean Martin, Shirley MacLaine, Arthur Kennedy

Kings Go Forth, 1958
Director: Delmer Daves
Cast: Frank Sinatra, Tony Curtis, Natalie Wood

A Hole in the Head, 1959
Director: Frank Capra
Cast: Frank Sinatra, Edward G. Robinson, Eleanor Parker, Carolyn Jones

Never So Few, 1959
Director: John Sturges
Cast: Frank Sinatra, Gina Lollobrigida, Peter Lawford, Steve McQueen

Can-Can, 1960
Director: Walter Lang
Cast: Frank Sinatra, Shirley MacLaine, Maurice Chevalier, Louis Jordan

Ocean's Eleven, 1960
Director: Lewis Milestone
Cast: Frank Sinatra, Dean Martin, Sammy Davis Jr, Peter Lawford, Angie Dickinson, Richard Conte, Cesar Romero

Pepe, 1960
Director: George Sidney
Cast: Cantinflas, Dan Dailey, Shirley Jones and guest appearance from Frank Sinatra

The Devil at Four O'Clock, 1961
Director: Mervyn LeRoy
Cast: Spencer Tracy, Frank Sinatra, Kerwin Matthews

Sergeants Three, 1962
Director: John Sturges
Cast: Frank Sinatra (also producer), Dean Martin, Sammy Davis Jr, Peter Lawford, Joey Bishop

The Road to Hong Kong, 1962
Director: Norman Panama
Cast: Bing Crosby, Bob Hope, Joan Collins, Dorothy Lamour and Frank Sinatra as unbilled guest star

The Manchurian Candidate, 1962
Director: John Frankenheimer
Cast: Frank Sinatra, Laurence Harvey, Angela Lansbury, Janet Leigh

Come Blow Your Horn, 1963
Director: Bud Yorkin
Cast: Frank Sinatra, Lee J. Cobb, Barbara Rush

The List of Adrian Messenger, 1963
Director: John Huston
Cast: George C. Scott, Dana Wynter, Clive Brook and Frank Sinatra in guest appearance

Four for Texas, 1964
Director: Robert Aldrich
Cast: Frank Sinatra, Dean Martin, Anita Ekberg, Ursula Andress, Charles Bronson

Robin and the Seven Hoods, 1964
Director: Gordon Douglas
Cast: Frank Sinatra (also producer), Dean Martin, Sammy Davis Jr., Peter Falk

None But the Brave, 1965
Director/Producer: Frank Sinatra
Cast: Frank Sinatra, Clint Walker, Tommy Sands, Brad Dexter

Von Ryan's Express, 1965
Director: Mark Robson
Cast: Frank Sinatra, Trevor Howard, Brad Dexter

Marriage on the Rocks, 1965
Director: Jack Donohue
Cast: Frank Sinatra, Deborah Kerr, Dean Martin, Cesar Romero

Cast a Giant Shadow, 1966
Director: Kirk Douglas
Cast: Senta Berger, Angie Dickinson and a guest appearance from Frank Sinatra

The Oscar, 1966
Director: Russell Rouse
Cast: Stephen Boyd, Elke Sommer, Milton Berle and Frank Sinatra in a guest appearance

Assault on a Queen, 1966
Director: Jack Donohue
Cast: Frank Sinatra, Virna Lisi, Tony Franciosa, Richard Conte

The Naked Runner, 1967
Director: Sidney J. Furie
Cast: Frank Sinatra, Peter Vaughan

Tony Rome, 1967
Director: Gordon Douglas
Cast: Frank Sinatra, Jill St John, Gena Rowlands, Richard Conte

The Detective, 1968
Director: Gordon Douglas
Cast: Frank Sinatra, Lee Remick

Lady in Cement, 1968
Director: Gordon Douglas
Cast: Frank Sinatra, Raquel Welch, Richard Conte

Dirty Dingus Magee, 1970
Director: Burt Kennedy
Cast: Frank Sinatra, George Kennedy, Anne Jackson

That's Entertainment, 1974
Director: Jack Haley Jr
Cast: Narrated by Fred Astaire, Bing Crosby, Gene Kelly, Peter Lawford, Frank Sinatra and others

Contract on Cherry Street (made for TV), 1977
Director: William A. Graham
Cast: Frank Sinatra, Jay Black, Martin Balsam, Harry Guardino

The First Deadly Sin, 1980
Director: Brian Hutton
Cast: Frank Sinatra, Faye Dunaway, David Dukes

Cannonball Run II, 1984
Director: Hal Needham
Cast: Burt Reynolds, Dom DeLuise and Frank Sinatra as himself

Who Framed Roger Rabbit? 1988
Director: Robert Zemeckis
Cast: Bob Hoskins, Christopher Lloyd and featuring the voice of Frank Sinatra as the cartoon character 'Singing Sword'

DISCOGRAPHY

This is not an exhaustive list of Sinatra's recordings but does include most and certainly the best records he has made during his long career.

1940 – 42
The Dorsey/Sinatra Sessions
RCA Victor
Six-album set

Includes: "The Sky Fell Down", "Fools Rush In", "You're Lonely and I'm Lonely", "I Could Make You Care", "Let's Get Away From It All", "Be Careful It's My Heart"

1942
We Three
RCA Victor

Includes: "Dig Down Deep", "The Lamplighter's Serenade", "Night and Day", "The Night We Called It a Day", "The Song is You"

1939 – 52
Sinatra Plus
Fontana
double album

Includes: "The Birth of the Blues", "The Nearness of You", "Bim Bam Baby", "One For My Baby", "All or Nothing at All", "All of Me", "Ol' Man River"

1939-52
The Essential Frank Sinatra
CBS
Three-album set

Includes: "From the Bottom of My Heart", "The Charm of You", "Nancy (with the Laughing Face)", "Everybody Loves Somebody", "It's Only a Paper Moon", "Why Try to Change Me Now"

1943 – 51
In the Beginning, Frank Sinatra
CBS
Two-album set

Includes: "I've Got a Crush on You", "The House I Live In", "The Moon was Yellow", "I Couldn't Sleep a Wink Last Night", "The Coffee Song", "Saturday Night (is the Loneliest Night of the Week)"

THE CAPITOL YEARS

1953 – 54
Songs for Young Lovers
Capitol

Includes: "The Girl Next Door", "They can't Take that Away from Me", "Violets for Your Furs", "Someone to Watch Over Me", "A Foggy Day", "I Get a Kick Out of You", "My Funny Valentine"

1953 – 5
Swing Easy
Capitol

Includes: "Jeepers Creepers", "Taking a Chance on Love", "Lean Baby", "I'm Going to Sit Right Down and Write Myself a Letter", "All of Me"

1955
In the Wee Small Hours
Capitol

Includes: "In the Wee Small Hours of the Morning", "Mood Indigo", "I Get Along Without You Very Well", "When Your Lover Has Gone", "This Love of Mine"

1956
Songs for Swingin' Lovers
Capitol

Includes: "You Make Me Feel So Young", "I've Got You Under My Skin", "Old Devil Moon", "Pennies Fron Heaven", "Makin' Whoopee", "Anything Goes"

1956
High Society
MGM Soundtrack

Includes: "High Society", "Who Wants to be a Millionaire", "True Love", "You're Sensational", "Well Did You Evah?"

1956
Close to You
Capitol

Includes: "Close to You", "PS I Love You", "With Every Breath I Take", "The End of a Love Affair"

1956
A Swingin' Affair
Capitol

Includes: "Night and Day", "I Wish I Were in Love Again", "I Got Plenty o' Nuttin'", "Nice Work if You Can Get It", "At Long Last Love", "You'd Be So Nice To Come Home To", "I Got it Bad and That Ain't Good", "From This Moment On"

1957
Pal Joey
Columbia Soundtrack

Includes: "There's a Small Hotel", "Bewitched", "The Lady is a Tramp", "I Could Write a Book", "Zip"

1957
Come Fly With Me
Capitol

Includes: "Come Fly With Me", "Moonlight in Vermont", "Let's Get Away From It All", "Blue Hawaii", "On the Road to Mandalay", "It's Nice To Go Trav'ling"

1957
Where Are You?
Capitol

Includes: "Where Are You?", "The Night We Called It a Day", "Maybe You'll Be There", "Autumn Leaves", "Baby, Won't You Please Come Home?"

1958
Only the Lonely
Capitol

Includes: "Only the Lonely", "Angel Eyes", "It's a Lonesome Old Town", "Blues in the Night", "Guess I'll Hang My Tears Out to Dry", "One For My Baby"

1958
Come Dance with Me
Capitol

Includes: "Come Dance With Me", "Something's Gotta Give", "Dancing in the Dark", "I Could Have Danced All Night", "Cheek to Cheek", "The Song is You"

1953 – 58
Look to your Heart
Capitol

Includes: "Look to Your Heart", "Not as a Stranger", "Our Town", "Same Old Saturday Night", "I'm Gonna Live Til I Die"

1959
Noone Cares
Capitol

Includes: "When No One Cares", "A Cottage for Sale", "Stormy Weather", "Why Try to Change Me Now", "I'll Never Smile Again"

1953 – 61
Frank Sinatra - 20 Golden Greats
Capitol

Includes: "That Old Black Magic", "Love and Marriage", "Fools Rush In", "The Lady is a Tramp", "All the Way", "Witchcraft, You Make Me Feel So Young", "Come Fly With Me", "High Hopes", "Let's Do It", "Young at Heart", "In the Wee Small Hours of the Morning"

1958 – 65
Sinatra for the Sophisticated
Capitol

Includes: "I Get a Kick Out of You", "Always, I've Heard That Song Before", "That Old Black Magic", "Baubles, Bangles and Beads", "Let's Get Away From It All"

1953 – 59
The Rare Sinatra
Capitol

Includes: "Don't Make a Beggar of Me", "Ya Better Stop", "Memories of You", "If It's the Last Thing I Do", "I Couldn't Care Less", "The One I Love (Belongs to Somebody Else)"

1960
Nice 'n' Easy
Capitol

Includes: "Nice 'n' Easy", "That Old Feeling", "How Deep is the Ocean", "You Go to My Head", "She's Funny That Way", "You Do Something to Me"

1960
Sinatra's Swingin' Session
Capitol

Includes: "When You're Smiling", "Blue Moon", "S'posin'", "It's Only a Paper Moon", "I Concentrate on You", "You Do Something To Me"

1957 – 60
All the Way
Capitol

Includes: "All the Way", "High Hopes", "Talk to Me", "To Love and Be Loved", "River, Stat 'way From My Door", "All My Tomorrows", "Sleep Warm"

1961
Come Swing with Me
Capitol

Includes: "Day by Day", "Sentimental Journey", "Almost Like Being in Love", "Five Minutes More", "Don't Take Your Love From Me", "Paper Doll, I've Heard That Song Before"

1957 – 62
Sinatra Sings . . . of Love and Things!
Capitol

Includes: "The Nearness of You", "Hidden Persuasion", "The Moon was Yellow", "I Love Paris", "Chicago", "Love Looks So Well on You", "Sentimental Baby", "I Gotta Right to Sing the Blues", "Something Wonderful Happens in Summer"

1962
Point of no Return
Capitol

Includes: "When the World was Young", "September Song", "There Will Never Be Another You", "It's a Blue World", "These Foolish Things", "As Time Goes By"

THE REPRISE YEARS

1960
Ring-a-Ding Ding!
Reprise

Includes: "Let's Fall in Love", "Be Careful, It's My Heart", "A Fine Romance", "In the Still of the Night", "Let's Face the Music and Dance", "You'd Be So Easy to Love", "I've Got my Love to Keep me Warm"

1961
Sinatra Swings
Reprise

Includes: "Falling in Love", "The Curse of an Aching Heart", "Don't Cry Joe", "Please Don't Talk About me When I'm Gone", "Love Walked In", You're nobody til somebody loves you

1961
I Remember Tommy
Reprise

Includes: "I'm Getting Sentimental Over You", "Imagination", "Daybreak", "Take Me", "It Started All Over Again"

1961
Sinatra and Strings
Reprise

Includes: "I Hadn't Anyone til You", "Misty", "Come Rain or Shine", "Prisoner of Love", "All or Nothing At All", "Yesterdays"

1962
Sinatra and Swingin' Brass
Reprise

Includes: "Goody Goody", "They Can't Take That Away From Me", "At Long Last Love", "Tangerine", "I Get a Kick Out of You", "Pick Yourself Up'

1962
Sinatra Sings Great Songs from Great Britain
Reprise

Includes: "The Very Thought of You", "We'll Gather Lilacs", "If I Had You", "A Nightingale Sang in Berkeley Square", "I'll Follow My Secret Heart"

1962
Sinatra-Basie
Reprise

Includes: "Pennies From Heaven", "Please Be Kind", "The Tender Trap", "My Kind of Girl", "I Only Have Eyes for You", "Nice Work If You Can Get It", "Learnin' the Blues"

1962
All Alone
Reprise

Includes: "The Girl Next Door", "Are You Lonesome Tonight?", "Indiscreet", "You Forgot to Remember", "The Song is Ended"

1963
The Concert Sinatra
Reprise

Includes: "I Have Dreamed", "My Heart Stood Still", "You'll Never Walk Alone", "Bewitched"

1963
Sinatra's Sinatra
Reprise

Includes: "I've Got You Under My Skin", "In the Wee Small Hours of the Morning", "The Second Time Around", "Young at Heart", "Call Me Irresponsible"

1964
Frank Sinatra Sings Days of Wine and Roses (and other Academy Award winners)
Reprise

Includes: "Days of Wine and Roses", "Moon River", "The Way You Look Tonight", "In the Cool Cool Cool of the Evening", "Secret Love", "Swinging on a Star", "The Continental", "Love is a Many Splendoured Thing"

1964
It Might as Well Be Swing
Reprise

Includes: "Fly Me to the Moon", "I Wish You Love", "I Can't Stop Loving You", "Hello Dolly", "The Best is Yet to Come", "Wives and Lovers"

1964
Softly as I Leave You
Reprise

Includes: "Emily", "Here's to the Losers", "Come Blow Your Horn", "I'm Losing You", "Then Suddenly Love", "Available", "The Look of Love"

1965
September of my Years
Reprise

Includes: "The September of My Years", "How Old Am I", "Last Night When We Were Young", "It Was a Very Good Year", "Hello Young Lovers", "September Song"

1965
Moonlight Sinatra
Reprise

Includes: "Moonlight Becomes You", "Moonlight Serenade", "Oh You Crazy Moon", "The Moon Got in My Eyes"

1965
Sinatra '65
Reprise

Includes: "Tell Her (You Love Her Every Day)", "Anytime at All", "My Kind of Town", "When Somebody Loves You", "Luck Be a Lady to Me"

1965
My Kind of Broadway
Reprise

Includes: "Everybody Has the Right to be Wrong", "Luck be a Lady", "Hello Dolly", "They Can't Take That Away From Me", "Have You Met Miss Jones?", "Without a Song"

1966
Strangers in the Night
Reprise

Includes: "Strangers in the Night", "Summer Wind", "Call Me", "On a Clear Day", "My Baby Just Cares for Me", "Downtown", "The Most Beautiful Girl in the World"

1966
Sinatra at the Sands
Reprise

Includes: "Come Fly With Me", "I've Got a Crush on You", "I've Got You Under My Skin", "Shadow of Your Smile", "One for My Baby", "Get Me to the Church On Time", "Angel Eyes", "My Kind of Town"

1967
Francis Albert Sinatra and Antonio Carlos Jobim
Reprise

Includes: "The Girl from Ipanema", "Quiet Nights of Quiet Stars", "Meditation", "I Concentrate On You", "Once I Loved"

1967
Francis A and Edward K
Reprise

Includes: "Follow Me", "Sunny", "Indian Summer", "Yellow Days", "Poor Butterfly", "Come Back to Me"

1964
Frank Sinatra and the World We Knew
Reprise

Includes: "Somethin' Stupid", "Don't Sleep in the Subway", "Born Free", "This is My Song", "Some Enchanted Evening"

1968
Cycles
Reprise

Includes: "Rain in My Heart", "From Both Sides Now", "Little Green Apples", "By the Time I Get to Phoenix", "Gentle On My Mind"

1968 – 9
My Way
Reprise

Includes: "Watch What Happens", "Didn't We", "Yesterday", "All My Tomorrows", "My Way", "If You Go Away"

1968 – 9
A Man Alone
Reprise

Includes: "A Man Alone", "Night", "Love's Been Good to Me", "Some Travelling Music"

1968 – 9
Watertown
Reprise

Includes: "Watertown", "Goodbye", "What a Funny Girl", "She Says", "Train"

1960 – 5
Frank Sinatra: A Man and His Music
Reprise

Includes: "Put Your Dreams Away", "All or Nothing at All", "The One I Love Belongs to Somebody Else", "Come Fly With Me", "How Little We Know", Ring-a-Ding Ding!", "Fly Me to the Moon"

1967 – 70
Sinatra and Company
Reprise

Includes: "Drinking Water", "Triste", "This Happy Madness", "One Note Sambe", "I Will Drink the Wine", "Lady Day"

THE COMEBACK YEARS

1973
Ol' Blue Eyes is Back
Reprise

Includes: "You Will Be My Music", "Nobody Wins", "Send in the Clowns", "Let Me Try Again", "There Used to be a Ball Park"

1973 – 4
Some Nice Things I've Missed
Reprise

Includes: "You Turned My World Around", "Sweet Caroline", "I'm Gonna Make it All the Way", "Tie a Yellow Ribbon Round the Ole Oak Tree", "You are the Sunshine of my Life", "What are You Doing the Rest of Your Life"

1973
Frank
Reprise

Includes: "Night and Day", "Come Rain or Shine", "It Might as Well be Spring", "Without a Song", "Polka Dots and Moonbeams", "It Started All Over Again"

1974
Sinatra - the Main Event
Reprise

Includes: "The Lady is a Tramp", "I Get a Kick Out of You", "I've Got You Under My Skin", "My Kind of Town", "My Way"

1963 – 75
Sinatra - the Reprise Years
Reprise
Four album set

Includes: "In the Still of the Night", "Granada", "I Get a Kick Out of You", "Fly Me to the Moon", "I've Got You Under My Skin", "Nancy", "The Way You Look Tonight", "All the Way", "Luck be a Lady", "Strangers in the Night", "What are You Doing the Rest of Your Life?"

1963 – 77
Portrait of Sinatra
Reprise
Double album

Includes: "Let's Face the Music", "All or Nothing at All", "My Kind of Town", "Call Me Irresponsible", "I Sing the Songs", "Young at Heart", "Somethin' Stupid", "Love's Been Good to Me"

1980
Trilogy (Past Present Future)
Reprise
Three album set

Includes: "The Song is You", "My Shining Hour", "More Than You Know", "Just the Way You Are", "McArthur Park", "Love me Tender", "What Time Does the Next Miracle Leave?", "Before the Music Ends"

1981
She Shot Me Down
Reprise

Includes: "Good Thing Going", "Thanks for the Memory", "Bang Bang (My Baby Shot Me Down)", "I Loved Her"

1984
L.A. is My Lady
Reprise

Includes: "LA is My Lady", "The Best of Everything", "Mack the Knife", "Stormy Weather", "If I Should Lose You", "After You've Gone"

1993
Duets
Capitol

Includes: "The Lady is a Tramp (with Luther Vandross)", "What Now My Love (with Aretha Franklin)", "Guess I'll Hang My Tears Out to Dry/In the Wee Small Hours of the Morning (with Carly Simon)", "I've Got You Under My Skin (with Bono)"

1994
Duets II
Capitol

Includes: a selection of Sinatra classics with Chrissie Hynde, Gladys Knight, Neil Diamond, Willie Nelson and others

INDEX